MEL BAY'S ~~COMPLETE~~ DULCIMER HANDBOOK

By Mark Biggs

Online Audio www.melbay.com/94047BCDEB

AUDIO CONTENTS

1	Give Me Your Hand [2:40]
2	Planxty Morgan Magan (O'Carolan) [2:47]
3	What if a Day [1:38]
4	Lord Inchiquin (O'Carolan) [2:57]
5	The Shepherds Hey [2:11]
6	Fuge in Bm [2:20]
7	Meagan Jayne/Planxty Irwin (M. Biggs/O'Carolan) [3:48]
8	Lass of Richmond Hill/Lass of Patie's Mill [2:27]
9	Red Haired Boy [2:33]

10	Maybe You'll Wander (M. Biggs) [2:21]
11	Jacky Tar [2:00]
12	Packington's Pound [2:41]
13	Lady Owen's Delight [2:12]
14	Planxty Fanny Power (O'Carolan) [2:35]
15	La Paloma [3:06]
16	Johnny I Hardly Knew You/Road to Lisdoonvarna/ When Johnny Comes Marching Home [3:20]
17	Improvisation on a Blue Mood [3:48]

Visit us on the Web at www.melbay.com — E-mail us at email@melbay.com

TABLE OF CONTENTS

SONG LIST:

MIXOLYDIAN SONGS

TWENTY-TWO SONGS (Intermediate to Advanced)

IONIAN AND NEW IONIAN SONGS

AEOLIAN SONGS

MARK BIGGS

Born in 1954 in Kansas City, Mark Biggs first began to play the Mountain Dulcimer in 1979 when he and a friend found a job playing music for free room and board in a small Greek restaurant on the south side of Crete. He's come a long way from those early "ad lib" days, winning many listener's ears and a growing national reputation along the way. The author of two books, THE MOUNTAIN DULCIMER (Mel Bay Publications) and the SEASON OF THE DREAM SONGBOOK, he has also recorded two record albums, NOT LICKED YET (Centennial Records-1981), and SEASON OF THE DREAM (Kicking Mule Records-221). Besides writing and recording for the dulcimer, he has taught hundreds of students around the Midwest: at workshops, at the Old Town School of Folk Music in Chicago, and through the Continuing Education Departments at Southwest Missouri State University and Drury College in Springfield, Mo. near where he currently makes his home on Table Rock Lake. He has also won many dulcimer championships, including:

1st Place (1984): National Mountain Dulcimer Championships in Winfield, Ks.

1st Place (1983 & 1981): Southern Regionals in Ark.

3rd Place (1983): National Championships in Winfield, Ks.

1st Place (1981): Ozark Mountain Championships in Mo.

1st Place (1980): Midwest Dulcimer Championships in Ia.

Mark has played and demonstrated the dulcimer to hundreds of thousands of people at Silver Dollar City (an 1880's theme park in S.W. Mo.) where he has worked for the past five years. When the season closes down for the winter, he can be heard in concert throughout the Midwest. If the opportunity arises, don't pass up the chance to hear his uniquely personal blend of traditional, jazz, and original dulcimer music.

For bookings, or to order any of his books, records or tapes, please write to him: C/O, R.R.#3 Box 367B/ Galena, Mo. 65656.

Photo by Mark Biggs

AUTHOR'S FOREWORD

It is my hope and intention that this dulcimer handbook will serve as a basic guide and source book for all dulcimer players, from the absolute novice to the most advanced picker. The **Whole Dulcimer Handbook** is meant to be used both as a songbook and as a lesson plan book, as a step-by-step guide to take you from the word go, on to an intermediate or advanced level with your mountain dulcimer.

Now before you say to yourself that such a feat is beyond your grasp, let me assure you that it is not. Every student that I have ever worked with who truly wanted to learn how to play their dulcimer has been able to do so, usually with far less difficulty than they had initially expected. All it takes to play the mountain dulcimer is desire and patience and perseverance. And even if you are currently happy playing your instrument in the traditional style with a noter, I still encourage you to read on and join in where you wish, for there will undoubtedly be plenty of information which you will find useful and hopefully inspiring as well.

Let me lay out concisely the three basic intentions of this handbook:

1. To increase your overall knowledge of the mountain dulcimer; to advance your understanding of modes and tunings, and in general of how the dulcimer operates.

2. To arm you with a greater degree of playing skill by looking at basic string techniques and by working through a series of strumming, finger and chord exercises designed to increase your dulcimer virtuosity. Along the way, we'll look at a group of familiar and unusual songs arranged to help you develop new and alternative playing styles.

3. To offer you a deeper insight into how music works in relation to yourself through your dulcimer. We'll look at the fundamentals of arranging songs and of improvising on the dulcimer; we'll learn how to place the chord structure of a song behind its melody line, and how to derive a melody line from the chord structure of a song. We'll learn how to transpose a song from one key to another so that it can be played more easily on your instrument. In short, we'll try to make playing the dulcimer simpler by coming to a better understanding of music in general.

NO WRONG OR RIGHT WAY TO PLAY THE MOUNTAIN DULCIMER

Let me make it clear from the beginning that the **Whole Dulcimer Handbook** is not to be taken for gospel. Rather it is meant to help you advance at your own pace in the direction your interests take you. There are no timetables, no tests, no deadlines to be met. Work through this book at your leisure using it as a reference guide to return to for information and inspiration throughout the years.

As far as I am concerned, there are no right or wrong ways to play the mountain dulcimer; only harder and easier means to reach the same ends. Because the dulcimer is a relatively recent invention, there exist no set playing styles, no decreed patterns to copy from or conform to; you are completely free to discover your own forms, or to carry on the traditional songs and playing styles. I have never met two dulcimer players who played exactly alike. Which is perfectly normal since no two people share identical interests, let alone the same finger span. The important thing to remember is this: to play your best you must be both comfortable with and engaged by your style. This means you must be both relaxed with and challenged by what you're playing. You must learn your own limitations and abilities, as well as your own interests and aspirations. A certain equilibrium or balance is necessary to play the dulcimer, and this means mentally as well as physically just to hold the slippery thing steady on your lap. The trick is to be both attentive and entertained; player and listener. Every bit of fresh technique, every new song builds on what you have already learned and becomes the ever growing foundation for your future efforts. Don't be afraid to make mistakes or to try something which seems outrageously difficult—the fact is you'll learn more by making mistakes than you ever will by repeating what you already know. Don't shy away from a new tuning or technique or some particularly difficult passage—what seems hard today will become easier tomorrow by your present efforts. And **above all else**, don't let your frustratiosn get the better of you. Relax and enjoy, and everyone else around you will also enjoy—that's the inherent nature of the dulcimer. **Remember there are no tried and true, wrong or right, sure fire ways to play the dulcimer; like everything else, the instrument is only as complex or as simple as you choose to make it.**

A BRIEF HISTORY OF THE MOUNTAIN DULCIMER

While there is considerable dispute concerning the dulcimer's history, it is generally accepted as one of the few true American instruments, first born and bred in the Appalachian Mountains along the Eastern seaboard in the early 1800's. Despite its probable American origin, the mountain dulcimer nevertheless remained pretty much in rural obscurity from the time of its birth clear up until the early 1960's when a renewed interest in folk music rescued it from near extinction. I'm happy to say that today the dulcimer is more widely recognized, built and played than ever before in its history.

Technically speaking the mountain dulcimer belongs to that family of instruments known as the plucked zither, and should not be confused with the **hammered dulcimer**, a large trapezoidal shaped, multi-stringed percussion instrument belonging to the psaltry family. Still the mountain dulcimer's "incorrect name" seems both readily explainable and appropriate. Undoubtedly the original builders were familiar with the repeated references to the "dulcimer" in their family Bible, and so would have been comfortable with this name.

Moreover the hammered dulcimer, our instrument's namesake cousin (and the dulcimer referred to in the Bible), was in vogue in New England at the time the mountain dulcimer was first being built in this country. So perhaps the mountain people named their "new instrument" after the already familiar hammered dulcimer, recognizing that both instruments shared a voice which was equally "sweet". And what could be more appropriate since the word dulcimer means "sweet song", coming from the Latin "dulce" for sweet, and the Greek "melos" for song or sound.

Historically a number of Renaissance instruments dating from the 1400's appear to form the basic model from which the mountain dulcimer evolved. The oldest direct ancestor seems to have been the German **scheitholt**, a small three or four stringed rectangular instrument played on the lap by running a wooden noter over the melody string. The scheitholt was either chromatic (12 toned) or modal (7 toned like the mountain dulcimer), and was tuned monochordally—all three or four strings tuned to the same note. This arrangement is still used on the mountain dulcimer today where it is most commonly called the "Bagpipe tuning". The scheitholt or "log zither" proved to be so popular that within a century it had begun to spread across Europe and Scandinavia where a series of new folk instruments began to evolve. Moving into France first, the scheitholt became the **Epinette des Vosges,** an instrument still played today. Later it migrated northward into Scandinavia where it changed shape and stringing arrangement to become the Swedish **humle,** the Norwegian **langeleik,** and the icelandic **langspil.** Back in continental Europe the scheitholt found its way into Holland where it became the **Hommel** (from the Dutch hommeln "to hum") or **humle.** All of these instruments were modal (some being altered into chromatic versions), and were played flat on the lap like the mountain dulcimer. Nonetheless, the mountain dulcimer's peculiar shape, tone, and stringing arrangement seem to mark it as a unique American contribution, more the result of a composite of these earlier European instruments than the direct descendant of any single relative. Or as Michael Murphy (to whom I am indebted for part of this brief history) writes in his book, the **Appalachian Dulcimer,** "It seems more likely that the dulcimer was an outgrowth of a variety of European instruments, created from the memory of the German, Norwegian, Dutch, and Swedish immigrants who settled in the Appalachians."

As I said at the beginning of this section there is no complete agreement about the origin of the mountain dulcimer. Mr. Stinson Behlen, a maker of dulcimers for 38 years with a long family history of being dulcimer luthiers, assures me positively that the first dulcimer was invented on the German-Dutch border in 1518 and was known as the "Nordish Balk". To date I have been unable to substantiate his assertions. And so being a dreamer and a "Show-me" Missourian, I continue to cherish the perhaps mistaken belief that the mountain dulcimer is in fact one of the few true American instruments.

BASIC PARTS OF THE DULCIMER:
Along With Some Repair & Buying Tips

Before we get into the meat of the matter, it seems best to begin by reviewing the names of the parts of our mountain dulcimer so that we can all speak the same language. Therefore let me lay out a diagram of the instrument:

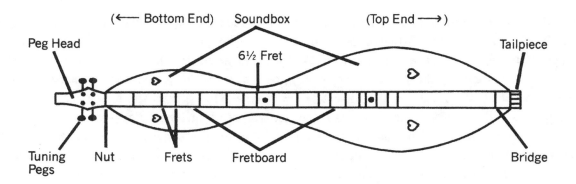

The most notable feature of the mountain dulcimer is its **fretboard** which unlike most other modern instruments runs the entire length of the dulcimer. The fretboard spans the whole **soundbox** and is responsible in large part for the very soft, sweet voice of the instrument. All the sound which the dulcimer produces must first pass directly through the fretboard into the soundbox before it can resonate back through the top and sides. It is therefore important that the fretboard be hollow or scalloped to allow as little vibrational resistance as possible—i.e. to give the dulcimer its loudest and sweetest voice. This is one thing you should be sure to look for when buying a dulcimer. The fretboard is divided into notes by thin metal bars called **frets.** To "fret" the instrument means to place your finger just to the left of the metal fret in order to play that note. Placing your finger directly over the fret will dull or mute the sound, while fretting too far to the left of the bar will sometimes cause a buzz or a dead note to be produced.

At the top end of the instrument we find the **bridge.** This small block of wood, plastic or ivory determines the height of our strings over the fretboard. The elevation of the strings is known as the **action** of our instrument and may be raised or lowered by changing the height of the bridge. The action should be light; you should not have to exert a great deal of pressure to fret your dulcimer to produce a good clean sound. If the action is too low you will probably get a buzzing sound when you fret certain notes on the fretboard. If the action is too high it will be difficult to fret the dulcimer, particularly at the top end of the fretboard, and may well cause these high notes to sound off pitch since you must bend the string too far down. I keep the action of my dulcimer set about one eighth of an inch above the 7th or octave fret. Please note that the height of your strings above the fretboard depends in part on how level your fretboard is. This is another thing you should check carefully when buying a dulcimer—sight along the fretboard and make sure it is either level or slightly bowed lower at the middle. If the fretboard bows up in the middle the dulcimer will be practically impossible to note clearly the entire length of the fretboard. To lower the action of your instrument carefully loosen the strings and cut the grooves in the bridge a little lower, checking every now and then to make sure you haven't lowered the action so much that you've created a buzz. An exacto knife with a fine blade or fine saw blade works well for this adjustment. On the other hand, if you have a widespread buzzing problem you probably need to raise the height of the grooves in your bridge. You can try cutting some new grooves next to the old ones, or you can have an instrument repairman put on a new bridge. If the buzzing problem occurs on just one fret more often than not the fret directly above or below the buzzing note will be the culprit. By **carefully** filing down the guilty fret with a fingernail file once you have located it, you can sometimes get rid of the buzz. You may want to file down just one side of the buzzing fret if the other two strings note cleanly, so check this possibility before filing the entire fret. Once again go slowly and check often to make sure you aren't lowering the fret too far. Occasionally, after much wear and tear and many hours of playing you will need to replace the old frets with new ones. This is a job any competent instrument repairman can do for a few dollars.

At the bottom end of the dulcimer is the **nut,** the equivalent of the bridge. Here too the string grooves should be neither too high nor too low (about ⅛") from the fretboard. Beyond the nut is the **peg head** or scroll with the tuning **pegs.** The pegs are the devices by which you tune your mountain dulcimer, lowering or raising the tension on the metal strings to produce a lower or higher pitch. There are three types of pegs: the traditional **friction peg** which is wooden and looks like a violin tuner; the modern equivalent to the friction peg known as the **precision peg** which is metal and works by means of a friction gasket; and the **geared peg** which uses a system of internal or external gears to create a more precise tuning mechanism. Friction pegs and precision pegs work on a one to one ratio—the string moves as far as you turn the peg—while geared pegs transfer the physical motion of the peg into a geared ratio on the order of a four to one or twelve to one. It is for this reason that I recommend geared tuning pegs—another thing to look for when buying a dulcimer. Certainly the precision pegs are much better than the old fashioned friction pegs which will inevitably cause you to break more strings and often prove practically impossible to fine tune. The friction peg may be more authentic, but believe me, musicians have always readily and joyfully accepted any mechanical advance which **makes** playing easier. So don't let someone sell you a dulcimer with friction pegs unless you know precisely what this will mean in terms of tuning.

PLAYING AND PICKING POSITIONS

Traditionally and still most frequently, the dulcimer is played flat on the lap. It is essential that you find a chair or stool which allows your feet to rest flat on the floor, leaving your thighs perfectly level. Otherwise the dulcimer will be forever slipping away from or towards you making it very difficult to concentrate on playing. Your legs must also be spread far enough apart to provide a good solid base for the instrument. As a general rule of thumb, the first fret should be centered in the middle of your leg, with the **sound holes** at the upper end of your dulcimer centered over your other leg. This position will prevent a distressing teeter-totter effect when you play the first and second notes. I also use a couple of small leather patches on my legs under the dulcimer to help stabilize the instrument. A piece of old chamois will work fine, or for you ladies who want to play in a dress, try draping a large chamois over your knees.

Proper Seating Posture

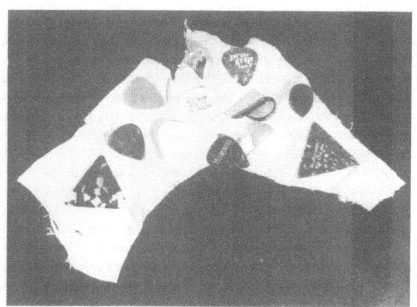

Assortment of Picks

Around the country a growing number of players are stringing a guitar strap under their legs to hold the dulcimer steady. They screw guitar buttons in either end of their dulcimer and attach the strap to these points. A number of progressive players stand up to play their dulcimers using the guitar strap strung around their neck and shoulders. If mobility is of the greatest concern to you this playing style may be of use, though you should be aware that it becomes increasingly difficult to play high up on your fretboard where your body and the strap begin to interfere.

Let's look at the **flat pick** for a few moments. Picks come in all different shapes and sizes, weights and thicknesses. The pick you choose is strictly a personal matter. I prefer a medium weight (.73 millimeter) nylon pick. I use Jim Dunlop picks (available in all good music stores) for a number of reasons. First, a nylon pick helps alleviate that bothersome click-click-clicking sound which a plastic pick makes as it strikes the side of the fretboard. Also you never have to worry about a nylon pick breaking, and several types have embossed or raised lettering on them which gives you something to hold on to. In time the pick will actually shape to your fingers and feel wonderfully natural in your hand. There are innumerable sorts and shapes of plastic picks if you prefer them. Or you can cut a pick out of a plastic butter dish top and shape it to your own design. Traditionally a goose quill was used to strum the dulcimer. This still makes for a lovely visual effect, though practically speaking they break apart pretty frequently, so be sure to keep a goose around the house if you want a constant supply of quills.

It is absolutely essential that we get started holding the pick in the proper way. **Hold the pick between the thumb and forefinger only.** They intersect at right angles with the ball of the thumb against the flat of the index finger; the pick is held in between these fingers, with its tip extending straight down from the forefinger's tip about 3/8ths of an inch. If the pick hangs down too far, you'll get a lot of pick noise from the tip striking the instrument; if too little pick extends, your fingers will hit and mute the strings.

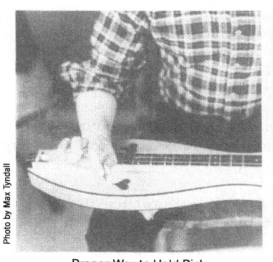
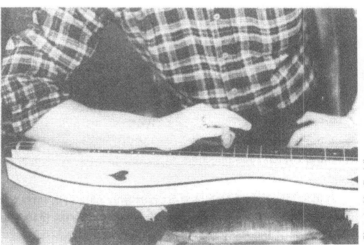

Photo by Max Tyndall

Photo by Max Tyndall

Proper Way to Hold Pick   Pick at Right Angle to Fretboard

To get into the proper picking position let's lay our right forearm down **directly on top of the fretboard** so that the pick's tip rests perpendicular, or at a right angle to the fretboard. The **strum is a gentle swing from the elbow,** as though you were wiping a piece of lint off your pant leg. **It is not a flip of the wrist or a push and pull from the shoulder,** but a gentle swing in both directions from the elbow so that the pick strikes the strings in a flat arc across the fretboard. If the wrist moves at all, it moves laterally, from side to side, not up and down in a flip flop motion.

This correct strumming motion means we will be picking down on the fretboard in the region of the 8th or 9th fret, instead of up at the **picking dip** near the bridge. **Picking down on the fretboard will not hurt your**

dulcimer and in fact will result in several positive effects besides forcing you to strum in the proper manner. First it will tend to mellow out the tone of your dulcimer. Next it will enable you to see both of your hands simultaneously (something you may find particularly useful when learning a new song.) And finally when we begin to study flat-picking and cross-picking techniques, you will be able to grab the side of the fretboard with your ring finger and give yourself a stable base to "pick a pattern" from.

In a few pages we will study our first strumming exercise, where we'll put all this picking information to good use. But first let's look at how to string the dulcimer and get tuned up together.

A FEW WORDS ABOUT STRINGS AND STRINGING

There is no definite stringing arrangement for the mountain dulcimer, in part because it is still a relatively young instrument. Usually the dulcimer has only three or four strings on it. The four stringed dulcimer in the Ozarks is commonly arranged so that the **melody string** (the string nearest to the player) is doubled up, leaving you with a variation of the three stringed dulcimer. The double strings are tuned to the same note and played as one string. Some players will spread the four strings on equal distance apart from one another. This arrangement is sometimes seen in the Appalachian Mountains and is particularly useful if you are a fingerpicker since it gives you one more string to play fingerpicking patterns on. If your dulcimer's nut and bridge don't have grooves already cut in them so that you can spread your strings four across evenly, you can cut the necessary two additional slots with an exacto knife. I have also seen five and six string dulcimers. Sometimes they will be double stringed clear across like a twelve-string guitar, sometimes they wlil be set up with a double first and three single strings. But, **for the purposes of this book we will be dealing with three stringed dulcimers,** (or four stringed instruments arranged with a double melody string.)

Just as there are no definitive stringing arrangements for the mountain dulcimer, there is no standard set of strings for the instrument. Since there are many different ways to tune the mountain dulcimer, as we will soon be discovering, the choice of which strings to put on your instrument will depend in part on what Mode or tuning you most commonly play in, as well as what key you normally tune into (how high or low you generally tune).

Since I typically play out of the Mixolydian Mode in the key of C (middle C on the piano) or D, I prefer to have a pronounced distinction between the tone of my melody and middle strings. Through trial and error I have found the following gauges work best on my dulcimer:

    Melody: two .10 gauge loop end strings
    Middle: one .14 or .15 gauge loop end string
    Bass: one .22 or .24 gauge wound string (phosphor bronze if available)

Every dulcimer will find its optimum voice with some certain mixture of string sizes. Do a little experimenting and try different sets to see what sounds best. A set of decent strings (such as the brand GHS) should last for about forty hours of playing, after which time they begin to rapidly lose their brilliance and ability to sustain a note.

You can buy "dulcimer string sets", though this usually means you are buying a set intended for the Ionian tuning, where the melody and middle strings share the same note. In such a packet you usually receive three .12 or .11 gauge strings, and one .21 nickel wound bass string. I prefer to find a nearby acoustic music store

14

which sells single strings. This way I can mix and match or buy single replacements. All you have to do is ask for the gauge string you want, in either "loop-end" or "ball-end" strings depending on what your dulcimer uses. You can tell by looking at how your dulcimer is currently strung. Ask for the gauge string you want from either the banjo bin if you use loop-end strings (don't let someone sell you mandolin strings for they're too short), or ask for single guitar strings if you need ball-end strings. Remember, the bigger the gauge you choose the deeper the tone. A heavier gauged set of strings should give your dulcimer a more bassy tone, but be aware that you will not be able to tune it as high as you could with a lighter set of strings. As I,said do a little experimenting to find what works best for you.

When you have to restring your dulcimer, don't panic. It will become a less frightening and time consuming task the more often you do it. Generally, you will need only two things: the strings and a small pair of wire snips or needle nose pliers. Stretch the replacement string from the point where it is secured (just the far side of the bridge) over the top of the fretboard to the peg you will be attaching it to. Now pull it past this peg by a good two inches and snip off the excess string with your wirecutters. This will prevent a big ball of worthless wire from gumming up your tuning peg. Be sure to remove the remainder of the broken string from around the peg, then slip your replacement string through the hole in the tuning peg so that about half an inch sticks out on the far side. Give the peg a couple of turns to get the string started around it, and then attach the loop end to the appropriate pin at the head of the dulcimer. (Needless to say, if your dulcimer uses ball-end string slip the string through the correct hole or guiding channel before measuring, clipping and attaching the string to the tuning peg.) Finally, tighten the string, making sure to get it into the proper slots in the bridge and nut, and then tune it up to the note you want. This will be a breeze in twenty tries, and seem self explanatory after the first time. Try to tighten both pegs on the same side of the peg head in the same direction so you'll always know which way to turn to tighten or loosen a string.

TUNING YOUR DULCIMER:
Plus A Few Words About Modes

The Modes:

The mountain dulcimer is a fundamentally different critter than the guitar or banjo, or just about any familiar modern instrument. Unlike these other instruments, **the dulcimer has no set tuning**. It is a **modal** instrument, rather than chromatic or 12 toned like most modern instruments; it represents a throwback to many medieval and Renaissance instruments which were 7 toned or modal in nature. Because the dulcimer is 7 toned, we never have all 12 notes of the chromatic octave present on our fretboard. As a result,there is no set tuning for the dulcimer since we must sometimes retune the instrument to find one of the missing chromatic notes.

Confusing, huh? You bet. When I first confronted the concept of a mode I panicked; it seemed as if there were nearly as many modes as I had toes. In time I discovered that I was wrong; there are in fact more modal tunings than my ten toes. Nevertheless, I managed in a short while to gain a firmer footing and greater understanding of the Modes, and learned how to tune my dulcimer easily through their many variations. So let me share what I have learned with you.

A Mode is basically an open tuning; a pre-established arrangement across the strings of your dulcimer.

There is a set, but flexible relationship between the melody, middle and bass strings. You can tune into any key you want within that preordained stringing arrangement; i.e.: as long as you know how to tune your strings so that you are in the Ionian, or the Mixolydian Mode, you can tune into the key of C, D, Eb, or whatever key you want to play a song in. Because each Mode has its own peculiar string arrangement, each Mode has its own characteristic sound (some major, some minor), and consequently each Mode utilizes different fingering positions to play the same chords. For instance: a C chord in the Ionian is fingered differently from a C chord in the Mixolyidian or Aeolian Modes.

There are seven different Modes, the names having been handed down to us from the Greeks who were using the modes thousands of years ago. Practically speaking, and fortunately for us, only four of the seven standard modes are used with any regularity today. They are the:

Minor Modes:	Major Modes:
Aeolian (A-O-lian)	Mixolydian (Mix-O-lid-ian)
Dorian (Door-ian)	Ionian (I-O-nian)

Note: Each of the **Standard Modes** can be slightly altered to become **New Modes**. A New Mode is one where you have switched the middle string and bass string notes. (We'll deal with them later in the book.)

Let me repeat for clearness:

1. **A Mode** is fundamentally: a seven note system, where the dulcimer's strings are arranged in a predetermined relationship.

2. **You can tune your dulcimer to any key in any mode,** though practically speaking you will find that the string gauges on your dulcimer will limit you to a four or five key range before they either break from too much tension, or buzz from slackness.

A mode can also be thought of as a pre-established series of whole and half-steps up your fretboard. Or as Neal Hellman writes, "A mode is a sequence of tones and semitones within a musical scale. Each mode has its own combination of tones and semitones (steps and half-steps)." In a chromatic octave we find 12 notes with a half step between each note.

Chromatic Octave:

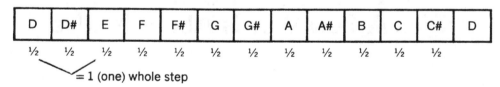

The Dulcimer's Fretboard:

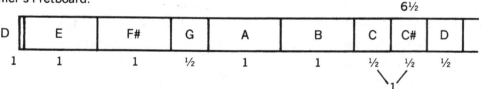

In the Modes the series of half and whole steps varies (diagram in Key of D):

Mixolydian Mode: 1   1   ½   1   1   ½   1   =   D E F# G A B C D

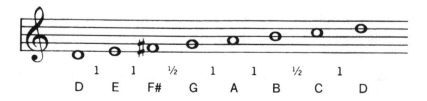

16

Ionian Mode: 1 1 ½ 1 1 1 ½ = D E F# G A B C# D

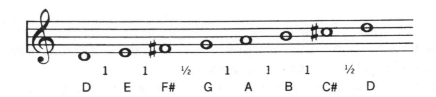

1 1 ½ 1 1 1 ½

D E F# G A B C# D

Dorian Mode: 1 ½ 1 1 1 ½ 1 = D E F G A B C D

1 ½ 1 1 1 1 ½

D E F G A B C D

Aeolian Mode: 1 ½ 1 1 ½ 1 1 = D E F G A Bb C D

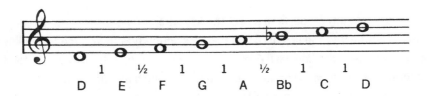

1 ½ 1 1 ½ 1 1

D E F G A Bb C D

NOTE: This step by half-step method of visualizing modes sometimes confuses me. But perhaps it will be of some use to you. Let me try to **forcefully correct one common misunderstanding:** You remain in the mode you have your open strings tuned into no matter what fret you start a song on. Even if you use a capo (a clamp which falls across all the strings and effectively retunes your dulcimer), you remain in the original mode until you retune your instrument. For instance, if you are in the Mixolydian Mode, key of D (strings tuned DD A D), and start a song on the third fret which happens to be a G note in this tuning, **you are not playing in the Ionian Mode,** rather you are playing a song in the key of G, out of the Mixolydian tuning. This is called **cross-keying.** We will discuss this possibility in greater detail later on. For now, suffice it to know that you can play in many different, but not all, keys out of any single tuning, in any single mode.

Many of you will be thoroughly confused by this point. Don't feel bad. Just remember where to find this section, for you will have cause to refer to it until the modal nature of the mountain dulcimer finally makes sense to you. For the present let's deal with just one Mode and get tuned up together so that we can stop theorizing and start playing.

TUNING INTO THE MIXOLYDIAN MODE:
Key of D

The Mixolydian Mode: A major mode associated with the sun, and so with lightness, by the Greeks. It has the distinctive characteristic of having a flattened seventh tone.

We will start this book off in the Mixolydian tuning for a number of good reasons. First, I find the Mixolydian to be the most flexible of all the different modes. It is a major sounding mode, less drone-like than the Ionian, well suited to a wide variety of songs both old and new. **Most importantly,** the chords can be easily inverted in the Mixolydian tuning by simply switching our finger positions on the melody and the bass strings. Also the Mixolydian mode offers us the option of walking a melody line across all three strings instead of always running it up and down the melody string as is traditionally done. These two very important considerations will eventually help us accomplish **one of the main goals of this book: namely to learn how to take a melody line and put the appropriate chord structure behind it.**

Tuning:

Step #1: The Melody String

The first step in tuning into any mode, is to select the **keytone**, the note corresponding to the key you wish to tune into. If you want to tune into the key of C, C is the note you'll tune to; to tune to the key of F select the tone F to tune to, and so on down the line. **NOTE:** You get this keytone note from any number of tuning aids—a pitch pipe; a tuning fork; an electronic tuner; another instrument such as the piano or the guitar (if you want to play with another instrument it is best to tune to that instrument); or you may simply tune to your voice, or to a tone which pleases your ears.

Once you decide on the keytone, tune one of the dulcimer's strings to that note. The string you choose to tune first will depend in part on habit (what has proven to be easiest in the past), and in part on which keytone you originally selected. **For the purposes of this book** however, accept that you will always tune your melody line string first. **We are going to tune into the key of D, in the Mixolydian Mode.** If you don't have another instrument to tune to (D above middle C on the piano—or to D the note on the 3rd fret of the 2nd string (the B string) of a guitar), you can buy a very inexpensive pitch pipe at a local music store. The D note on a Tenor Banjo tuning pipe works nicely. Now tune the melody string of your dulcimer to D (D above middle C)—listen carefully to your source for this keytone and bring your string up or down accordingly to this tone.

There are two essential ingredients to tuning: 1.) Take your time—don't rush; 2.) Listen carefully to what you are doing at all times. Be sure to **constantly pluck the string you are tuning so that you can hear where you are and where you are going.** You may find it easier in the beginning to lower your string well past the intended note and then tune up to it gradually. There will often be a **dead zone** in a tuning peg—a slack area where the peg is turning but nothing is happening. Pass through this dead zone quickly, don't get hung up in it thinking you are tuning—you'll be able to hear the tone of your string going up or down when you are actually tuning as long as you are striking the string every second or so. **Listen carefully,** you will be able to hear the sound of your string converging on the keytone. Visualize in your mind's ear two (tone) points coming together (like bringing your two forefingers together). When they touch, when your string is at the same pitch as your keytone source, there will be a full bodied harmony or resonance sounding out where a brief moment before there was a slightly strident or discordant sound existing between your string and the keytone. Be patient and practice listening. The only way to learn to tune is to do it over and over again until you can hear the very slight differences in tones which really do exist. No, you are not tone deaf or you wouldn't have the least interest in music or in learning to play your dulcimer.

If you have a double melody string, tune the second string to the same tone as the first melody string.

Step #2: The Middle String

Now come up to the third (3rd) fret on your middle string. Remember 0 is the open string, 1 = the first fret, 2 = the second fret, and so on. (**Note:** If you were formerly tuned in the Ionian Mode chances are you will have to lower the tone on your middle string at this point, so don't twist up and break a string. Lower the tension and work back up to the tone you're after.) When you are at the third fret on the middle string, hold it down and **tune the middle string to the same tone as that of your first string played open.** Again be patient and persevering.

If you are uncertain whether you need to raise or lower the pitch of your middle string, try this simple test. If moving up the fretboard from the third fret to the 4th, 5th, 6th, or on to a higher fret brings you closer to a tone roughly equivalent to that of the melody string played open, then you need to **raise** the tension on your middle string (i.e.: tune up the middle string). If you find that you must move down the fretboard to the 2nd, 1st, or to the open middle string in order to approach the tone of your open melody string, then you need to **lower** the tension of your middle string (tune down the middle string).

Step #3: The Bass String

Once the middle string is tuned to the melody string, we have a choice as to how to tune the bass string. So let's use both possibilities and give ourselves a fail-safe device. Come up to the fourth (4th) fret on the bass string (the string farthest away from you), and **tune the bass fretted at the fourth to the tone of the open middle string.** When you are satisfied that the bass and middle string share the same tone, **come up to the seventh (7th) or octave fret on the bass string and make certain that its tone is exactly the same as that of the melody string played open.** If there is a difference in tone between the bass string fretted at the seventh and the melody string played open, start over with the middle string and make sure you have the proper tone on it. Of course you can always go straight to the 7th fret on the bass and tune the bass first to the open melody string, then double check it at the fourth against the middle string. (If you can't get all three strings in tune using these instructions get a musically inclined friend to try, and if they still can't tune your dulcimer, you may have a faulty instrument.)

For review: First we select the "keytone", then we tune the melody string to this same pitch. Next we fret the middle string at the third fret and tune it to the open melody string. Finally we fret the bass at the fourth fret and tune it to the open middle string, double checking it by fretting it at the seventh fret and making sure it now has the same tone as the melody string played open. You are now in the Mixolydian Mode.

Don't be timid when tuning. You are the only one who can make music with your instrument—it will never play itself. You must take charge. You are bound to break a few strings; that's part of playing a stringed instrument. In time the cold sweat which some of you may experience when tuning or restringing your dulcimer will disappear. The secret lies in practice, patience and listening.

Graphically the Mixolydian Mode looks like this (remember we can tune any Mode into any "key" we wish):

Mixolydian Mode: Melody	Middle	Bass	(Key)
DD	A	D	(D)
CC	G	C	(C)
EE	B	E	(E)
(1)	(5)	(8)	

In terms of piano relationships, the pattern which the Mixolydian Mode always builds on is a 1 to 5 to 8 arrangement (where 1 and 8 are one octave apart, 8 being lower in tone.)

When we are ready to tune into the other modes later on, we will repeat this tuning explanation for each Mode. Until then we will deal exclusively with the Mixolydian Mode. **Note** however, that the rhythm and chord exercises we are about to study can be used for any modal tuning. Likewise with the finger exercises, though here it is important to remember that the cross-over points between strings will change for each Mode.

BASIC RHYTHM AND STRUMMING EXERCISES: Exercise #1

Generally speaking, there are two basic elements in music: melody and rhythm. The melody is a succession of notes strung together to represent the song's story line—it is carried up and down and across the fretboard. The rhythm is the timing of the song; it determines how long a count we give each note in the melody line, and how many beats each measure of music receives. It is the pace at which the story line unfolds.

On the dulcimer our picking or strumming hand (the one holding the flat pick) assumes the task of maintaining a song's rhythm and tempo. As with any stringed instrument, our two hands are doing entirely different things—in effect we are rubbing our bellies and patting our heads. So again be patient with yourself. It takes a while to get both hands working together, and both hemispheres of your brain humming in harmony. Though eventually both hands must work together, I have found it most helpful for the beginner to attack their two hands separately. So we will look first at the rhythm hand, your right hand if you are right-handed, or vice-versa if you are left-handed and your dulcimer is strung backwards. **The following exercise should become part of your standard warm-up; do it every time you sit down with your** dulcimer and in no time you will feel far more relaxed and in much better control of your strumming.

Let's begin with a simple four-four rhythm (perhaps the most common time signature). **Note:** There are many different time signatures: 4/4, 2/4, 3/4, 6/8, 6/4, etc. The time signature given at the beginning of every song tells you how many beats you have per measure of music—in a 4/4 song you have four evenly spaced counts per measure. For more information on time signatures see the proper appendice at the back of this book.

We will begin by strumming each stroke away from us. Don't worry about using your noting hand at all right now; don't do anything with it for the time being. Get your foot tapping to the 4/4 beat and count out loud (don't be shy, these two things will help you keep a steady rhythm going, which is exactly what you are trying to do here). When you are comfortable strumming with all strokes heading away from you, then reverse direction and bring all the strokes towards yourself. **If you have forgotten the proper way to hold the pick, and the correct strumming motion or position, go back and immediately review them in the Picking and Strumming section.** Again when you are comfortable bringing all the strokes towards yourself, start strumming in both directions: a stroke away followed by one towards yourself. (Note: Don't stop at this point; go directly from strumming only towards yourself to strumming both directions). When you are comfortable go into double time, exactly twice as many strokes in the same amount of time, strumming in both directions once again. **Double time is counted: one and, two and, three and, four and. So you will be strumming away from yourself on the one, two, three, four counts and towards yourself on the "and" counts.** When you are comfortable with the double time strum, go back into the single time (the original beat) strumming away from and towards yourself. Then fall back into strumming all towards yourself, and end up by strumming all away from yourself.

Graphically the strumming exercise looks like this:

4/4: ↑↑↑↑ / ↓↓↓↓ / ↑↓↑↓ // ↑↓↑↓↑↓↑↓ // ↑↓↑↓ / ↓↓↓↓ / ↑↑↑↑

Practice this basic exercise every day. If you feel weaker strumming one direction or another, then concentrate on bringing that strumming direction under control.

FINGER EXERCISE #1:
Finger Warm-ups & Scale Practice

Now that we've tuned up together and have finished our first basic rhythm exercise let's move directly on to our first finger or melody exercise. This exercise is intended to do two basic things: 1.) To limber up your fingers and give them greater flexibility, strength, and suppleness. 2.) To familiarize you with the whole fretboard; to show you where all the notes are on all the strings so that you can begin to see where convenient "cross-over" points exist between the strings.

Let's begin with the basic exercise and walk up the fretboard to discover the major scale of the key we are tuned in. Be sure to use all of your fingers. Remember we are in the Mixolydian Mode, key of D, so we will be walking a D-major scale. **We start on the melody string from the open position and proceed:** 0 (the open melody string), to the 1st fret, to the 2nd, 3rd, 4th, 5th, 6½ fret, and end on the 7th or octave fret. If your dulcimer does not have the 6½ fret you can find this same note at the 9th fret on the middle string. I strongly urge you to have the 6½ fret put on your dulcimer by a competent instrument repairman and to be certain to look for it when buying a new dulcimer. Without this fret it is impossible to play a major scale from the open position, and very difficult to play many songs—I will make constant use of the 6½ fret throughout this book as do most contemporary dulcimer books.

In diagram, this finger exercise looks like this (follow the numbers up and down):

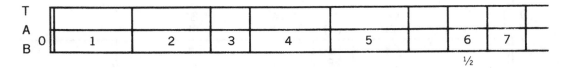

In the Mixolydian Mode this pattern gives you the major scale of whatever key you are tuned in, the key being determined by the open note found on your melody string. To walk the scale back down from the octave or 7th fret we simply retrace our steps back down the fret board.

When you are comfortable with this finger warm-up, let's walk across the three strings of our dulcimers utilizing this same scale once again. This time we will begin on the bass string from its open position, and walk up the string: 0, to the 1st fret, 2nd, 3rd; then switch to the middle string: 0, to the 1st fret, 2nd, 3rd. This time the diagram looks like this:

0	1	2	3
T 4 | 5 | 6 | 7 | | |
A
B | | | | |

Again to reverse the scale we simply start at the 3rd fret on the middle string and walk the pattern backwards. **This pattern gives you exactly the same scale one octave lower than the scale which we played on the open melody string a moment ago.**

When we move from the 3rd fret on the bass string to the open middle string we are making use of a **cross-over point.** We "cross-over" between strings whenever we move from one string to another without repeating the same note we just played. In other words as we walk our scales across the three strings we search for points which enable us to move smoothly and logically from one string to another without ever repeating a note, and without ever having to make long or awkward jumps along the fretboard.

Now then let's put both of these scale patterns together and walk across and up the fretboard through two complete octaves. We'll use numbers going up and the names of the notes which these numbers correspond to when we walk the pattern back down. Follow the diagram, and begin on the open bass string using the fingers marked: (L = little finger, R = ring finger, M = middle finger, I = index finger)

0	1L	2R	3M					
T 4	5L	6R	7M					
A	8L	9R	10M	11I	12R		13M	14I
B								

(in reverse)

D	E	F#	G					
T A	B	C#	D					
A	E	F#	G	A		B	C#	D
B								

Finally let's run this scale up and down one more time, looking at a different set of cross-over points. We climb up the fretboard exactly as above, but fall back down following a new set of numbers (using the fingering indicated):

D 14	E 13L	F# 12L	G 11R	A 10M	B 9I			
T			C# 8L	D 7R	E 6M	F# 5I		
A B				G 4L	A 3L	B 2R	C# 1M	D 0I

Practice these fingers warmups along with the rhythm exercises we ran through a moment ago whenever you sit down to play your dulcimer. Together the two exercises will help get you limbered up and ready to play. This one in particular will loosen up your fretting fingers, and more importantly it will teach you to hear a major scale (which happens to be one of music's basic building blocks). **The dulcimer is an easy instrument to get started playing and to pick out simple melodies on precisely because its fretboard lays out the major scale for you.**

HOW TO READ DULCIMER TABLATURE

The numerical tabs in this book are written for a traditional three string dulcimer. (Note: The double first string is counted as a single course or string.) So the three lines of tablature staff presented below the musical score of each song relate directly to the strings of your dulcimer as they appear when you are playing your instrument. **Reading down vertically,** the top number corresponds to the fret position played on the bass string, the middle number to the fret position on the middle string, and the bottom number (the one nearest to you) applies directly to the fret position on the melody string.

```
                          2
BASE COURSE   T ———————————————————
                          3
MIDDLE        A ——————————————————————— D chord (Mixolydian D)
                          4
MELODY        B ———————————————————
```

To play the tab as indicated, push down the appropriate string **just to the left** of the indicated fret. When you encounter a 0 this means the string is to be played open. If no number is given at all the choice to play the string is yours. **If you see an "X", this means the string is not to be played.** Throughout this book I merge the melody line together with the song's chord structure. **If the full two or three fingered tablature is too difficult for you, the bottom line of the tab will represent the melody line 90% of the time.** This means you can play the song in a traditional style by simply fingering the bottom number of the tab and strumming the middle and bass string open. By all means construct your own arrangements for these songs. You can play them as they are written, or play them using partial chords (using two of the three tab numbers), or you can develop your own unique fingerings which is why I give you the melody line note with the appropriate chord structure above, as well as the dulcimer tablature below.

LESSON #1: Placing Partial Chords Behind The Melody Line

Let's put what we have learned so far to use, and begin to weave the melody line of a simple song together with its chord structure. This method of playing will give your dulcimer a fuller, richer sound a bit more like what we commonly hear coming from the guitar or the piano. For this lesson we will begin by learning a familiar song, then see how to place two kinds of partial chords together with that melody. These partial chords, known as the **split octave chord** and the **set chord,** employ just two fingers and can be easily used with any song which you already play in the Mixolydian Mode. Let's start with a song we all know, Stephen Foster's classic, "Oh Susanna".

Learning the melody line should always be your first step when approaching a new song. The melody line will tell you several important things immediately. First and foremost, it will let you see whether you want to invest the time and energy necessary to learn the song. Don't waste your time working with songs which don't move or interest you. You will be living with them for a long time, so be choosey. Secondly, the melody line will give you some immediate insight into the timing and phrasing of the song, and so get you started with the rhythmic half of the piece. Finally, the melody line will show you how the notes move up and down the fretboard and consequently, it will give you an idea of when and where you will later be able to conveniently work in some chords behind the melody.

Let's begin by going through the unadorned melody line of "Oh Susanna", playing it in the traditional style, straight up and down the first string. It looks like this:

"Oh Susanna"

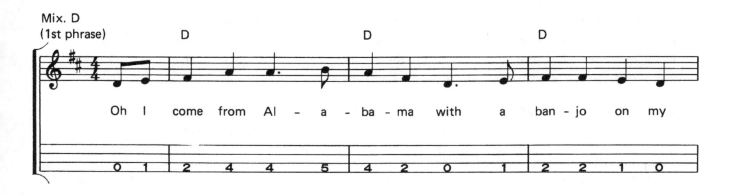

Playing the melody on the first string of your dulcimer in this manner allows the middle and bass strings to ring in a constant droning D chord (the open strings being the notes **A** and **D** respectively, representing two thirds of a full D chord which is made up of the notes: D, A, F#). This droning style is the traditional way of playing with a noter, or wood bar.

As you play through "Oh Susanna" several times, take notice of the four phrases and two parts which the song is divided into. **If you will break a new song down into its phrases, you will be able to learn the song more quickly and easily.** In this case, we find the first phrase followed by a second phrase which is identical to it, except for the last three notes. The first phrase ends: 1, 0, 1, while the second phrase ends: 1, 1, 0. The third phrase can be thought of as the second part of the song since it bears no relationship to the first or second phrase. Finally we discover a fourth phrase which is exactly the same as the second phrase. So all we really have to remember is that we have a first phrase (sequence of melody notes), followed by a second phrase (nearly the same as the first), backed by a second part and ending with a fourth phrase which happens to be identical to the second phrase. Maybe this sounds complicated to you on paper, but try applying the method to any new song as you play through it and see if it doesn't make good sense. Every song is made up of a sequence of phrases and parts. If you can discover this order, you can make it much easier to learn and memorize any tune.

Once we have learned our melody line, we can begin to immediately add two basic partial chords to any song we play in the Mixolydian Mode. The first and easiest of these techniques is known as the **split octave** chord. We form this two finger chord by reaching across and doubling up on the bass string, exactly duplicating the melody note which we are playing on the melody string. This split octave technique takes advantage of the octave division which exists between the melody and bass string in the Mixolydian Mode. **In effect we play the melody on the melody string and the bass string simultaneously by fretting the first string with our index finger and the bass string with our middle finger.** You can also use your thumb on the melody string and first finger on the bass string. **Do not try to note the bass string with your index finger and the melody string with your middle finger** for this reverse fingering forces your arm and elbow into your body and prevents you from walking the split-octave chord up the fretboard with ease. Here's what the **split-octave** variation looks like:

"Oh Susanna" - Split Octave Chord

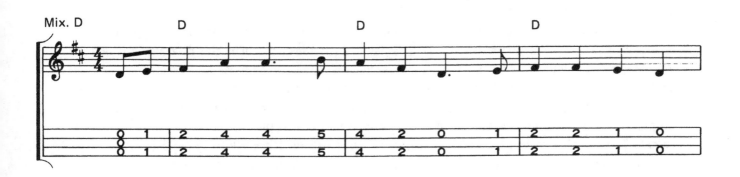

Playing through "Oh Susanna" with the split octave technique should also show you that **in the Mixolydian Mode you can play the melody line of any song on the bass string alone.** This gives you another possible variation for arranging a song or for when you play with other dulcimer players.

The second two finger chording technique which can be used with any song played in the Mixolydian Mode is called the **set chord.** It is so called because the middle finger will be used as a set or stationary pivot point on the middle string while we continue to walk the melody line up and down the melody string. This technique is a bit more difficult than the split octave chord, but it is essential to learning how to place the full chord structure behind the melody line later on. It is also the basic move you will use in a few moments to invert certain chords as you walk them up and down the dulcimer's fretboard.

When you begin to use the "set chord" it becomes imperative that you know the way the melody line moves up and down the fretboard. This will determine in part where your set chords will be formed and what fingers we will assign to which notes (or frets) above and below the pivot point of the set chord. "Oh Susanna" uses only one set chord position, but some songs will utilize three, four or more set positions on the middle string. We'll work with several such songs in a moment. For now, your set chord position can be found at the third fret on the middle string. Use your middle finger to fret this set chord position, then assign your little finger to the 1st fret on the melody string, your ring finger to the 2nd fret, your index finger to the 3rd, 4th and 5th frets on the melody string. You can just as easily use your thumb for the fourth and fifth frets if it feels more comfortable. Having figured out which fingers go where, let's walk through "Oh Susanna" several times using the "set-chord" technique:

"Oh Susanna"- Set Chord

Finally, here is what "Oh Susanna" looks like when we use all three techniques to play the song. (Note: This is only one possible way to arrange the song. By mixing and matching techniques you are beginning to learn how to **arrange** a song. Look at "The Camptown Races" for another example.)

Remember, you are in control of your dulcimer. It will only respond to your touch; no matter how hard you may will it, the instrument will never play itself. Remember also, as far as I am concerned **there are no wrong or right ways to play the dulcimer, only easier and harder ways to reach the same end.** Discover for yourself what works best for you, always keeping in mind that what you do one instant directly affects what you will have to do the next moment.

Photo by Mark Biggs

"Oh Susanna" - Combined Arrangement

Oh! Susanna

I come from Alabama with a banjo on my knee,
I'm going to Louisiana my true love for to see.
It rained all night the day I left,
the weather it was dry,
The sun so hot I froze to death;
Susanna don't you cry.

Oh Susanna, oh don't you cry for me,
I come from Alabama with a banjo on my knee.

I had a dream the other night when everything was still,
I thought I saw Susanna, a-coming down the hill.
The buck-wheat cake was in her mouth,
The tear was in her eye,
Say I, I'm coming from the South,
Susanna don't you cry.

Oh Susanna, oh don't you cry for me,
I come from Alabama with a banjo on my knee.

Photo by Mark Biggs

"The Camptown Races"

Stephen Foster 1850

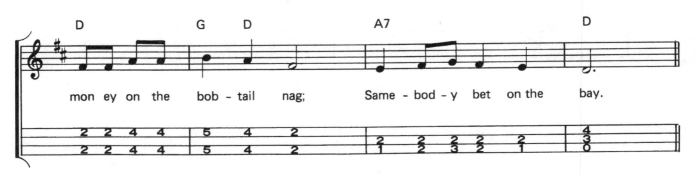

33

RHYTHM & STRUMMING EXERCISE #2:
(4/4 Time)

Chord Inversions in the Mixolydian Mode

As mentioned earlier in the section concerning "Modes", one of the most useful things about the Mixolydian Mode is the ability to quickly and easily invert most chords by simply switching our finger positions on the melody and bass strings. Because the melody and bass string share the same note exactly one octave apart in this tuning, when you move your melody line finger directly across to the corresponding fret on the bass string, and simultaneously move your bass string finger across to the identical melody string fret, you have "inverted" the chord. Inverting a chord works like this:

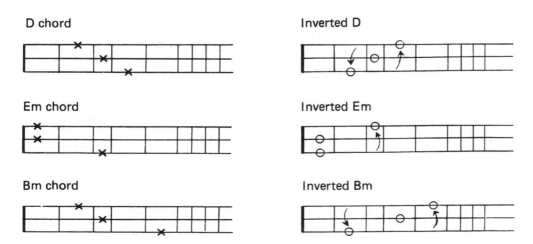

D chord	Inverted D
Em chord	Inverted Em
Bm chord	Inverted Bm

Let's use this ability to invert chords and put it together with our first basic rhythm exercise (p. 21) to form our second rhythm exercise. Here we will be inverting a chord every time we alternate our strumming direction. We will be using the D and Em slant (\) chord forms:

D   Em

Start with the D chord in its primary position (shown by the X's) and strum all the strokes away from you in a nice slow steady 4/4 rhythm. When you change picking directions and begin to bring the strokes all towards you, simultaneously invert the D chord (go to the O position). When you begin to strum in both directions, simultaneously slide the inverted D chord up the fretboard into the inverted Em chord form (the O marked form); without lifting your fingers slide up towards the bridge one fret per finger. As you go into double time (picking both directions), invert the Em chord to form the primary Em chord (Em marked by X's). When you drop from the double time stroke back into the original tempo (picking both directions), also move the Em chord back into the orignal D chord from. Now bring the strokes all towards you, and once again invert the D chord. Finally, end by strumming all the strokes away from you in the original 4/4 time, simultaneously inverting back into the original D chord. The exercise looks like this:

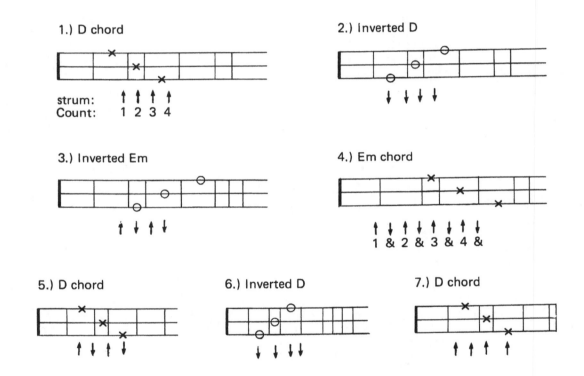

1.) D chord

strum: ↑ ↑ ↑ ↑
Count: 1 2 3 4

2.) Inverted D

↓ ↓ ↓ ↓

3.) Inverted Em

↑ ↓ ↑ ↓

4.) Em chord

↑ ↓ ↑ ↓ ↑ ↓ ↑ ↓
1 & 2 & 3 & 4 &

5.) D chord

↑ ↓ ↑ ↓

6.) Inverted D

↓ ↓ ↓↓

7.) D chord

↑ ↑ ↑ ↑

You can easily repeat this exercise using either of the other two invertable chord forms shown above. This exercise is designed specifically to get both of your hands working together, and to begin to acquaint you with chord inversions and how to slide from one chord into another with ease. **Note:** The set chord work we did with "Oh Susanna" formed the basis for the pivotting we use in this exercise to invert the D and Em chords. Let's look at the set chord technique one more time, now recognizing its importance for future chord inversions.

LESSON #2: Set Chords in "Swanee River"

Once again let's work with a well known Stephen Foster song, "Swanee River", paying particular attention to the use of set points on the middle string. Unlike "Oh Susanna" which used only one set point, "Swanee River" utilizes four set positions. As before we'll begin by learning the melody line of the song.

Remember to break the song down into its phrases and parts to make it easier to learn. You should be able to associate set positions with these phrases and thus in turn make it easier to remember the correct set chord movements in the song. Here's how "Swanee River" looks with its set chords.

Remember that you can also use the "split octave" partial chord, or simply play the melody line on the bass string. Before moving on let's look at the set chord and split octave techniques in a another context, by playing through the classic dulcimer tune, "The Wildwood Flower".

"Old Folks At Home", or "Swanee River"

Stephen Foster 1851

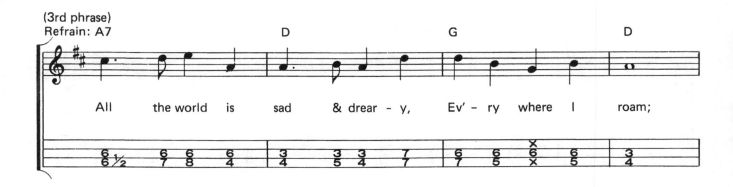

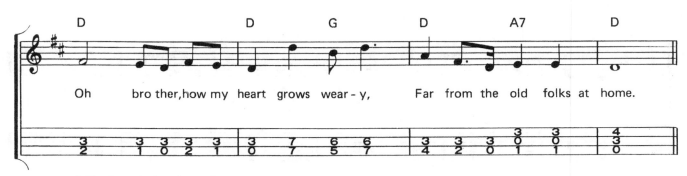

* X = do not play the string

37

"Wildwood Flower"
(Set Chord Form)

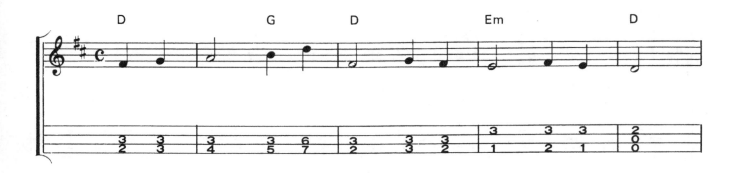

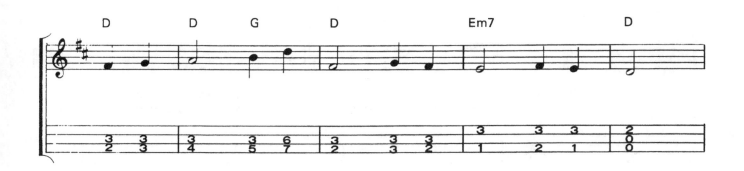

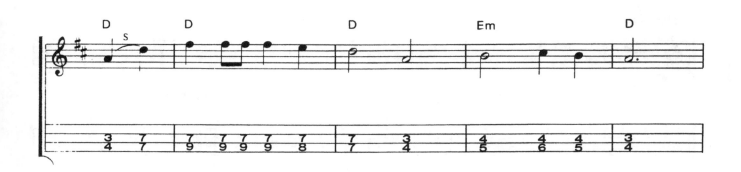

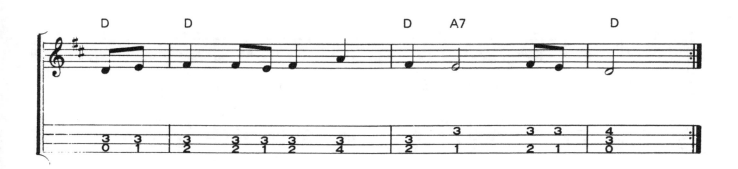

"The Wildwood Flower"
(Split Octave Form)

TWO FINGER HARMONY CHORDS: 3RDS & 5THS

The dulcimer is particularly well suited to playing harmonizing notes behind a melody line. In the Mixolydian Mode we can draw on our knowledge of set chords to see how easy it is to place harmony notes behind any melody line. This technique often gives the melody an unusual and pleasant sound. It will be easiest to use fretboard diagrams to show you how to put a harmony note behind the melody. These partial chords won't sound good with every song, but they should be kept in mind as one more possible way to arrange the songs you know.

3rds: (Here as always chords are grouped by symbols)

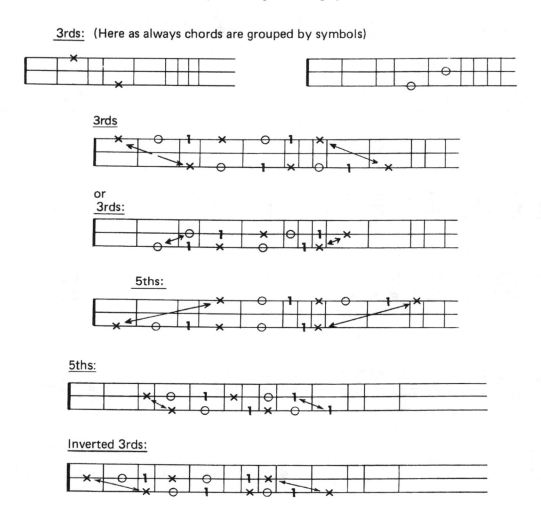

3rds

or
3rds:

5ths:

5ths:

Inverted 3rds:

Before we move on to use 3rds and 5ths in a couple of songs, let's work through two finger exercises built around third and fifth intervals.

FINGER EXERCISE #2:
3RD & 5TH INTERVALS

These exercises will limber up your fretting fingers, and should help you hear the natural intervals and transition points which occur between notes located a third (two full steps) apart and a fifth (three and 1/2 steps) apart. These intervals should make perfect sense to your ears since they are commonly used in western music. In fact if you arbitrarily select a note (the tonic) and place the notes positioned a third and a fifth above it you will have built the major chord named after the tonic or original note: i.e., if you start with a D note and put the third (F♯) and the fifth (A) together with the D, you will have built a D-chord.

Third and fifth intervals are often used to build melodies, and to improvise lead lines. As you work through the exercises below, listen carefully and try to begin to hear and relate the notes located a third and a fifth apart from one another.

Finger Exercise #2: 3rd Intervals

5th Intervals

3rd & 5th Intervals

43

Lesson #3: Using 3rds in "La Paloma" & "Sonya's Song"

The harmonies created by 3rds form one of the most pleasant sounds. Here is a lovely Spanish folksong written by Sebastian Yraider in the middle 1800's which makes good use of thirds to give this classic tune, "La Paloma", that south of the border feel it so rightly demands. If you wish to play only the melody line, follow the bottom tab except where the melody line crosses over to the middle string (marked by X's in the melody line tab.) Later in the advanced song section of this book we'll look at "La Paloma" played with full chords placed behind the melody line.

I've also included one of the first pieces I ever wrote, composed shortly after the birth of my youngest niece, and so named after her. "Sonya's Song" makes extensive use of both straight and inverted thirds. As always, the easiest way to learn this song is to break it down into its main parts and from there into the phrases which form each part. This I have done for you to help you see the main parts. "Sonya's Song" can be heard on both the Mel Bay tape, **Mountain Dulcimer,** and on the album, **Not Licked Yet.** **La Paloma** may be heard on the Mel Bay tape, **Complete Dulcimer Handbook,** which accompanies this book.

44

Once a well respected and highly successful Spanish composer, Sebastian Yradier lived from 1808 to 1865. "La Paloma" is perhaps his best loved, and certainly one of his longest lived songs. Part of its enduring nature comes from its use by Bizet in his Opera, "Carmen". This song has all the fire and spice of the Spanish, so play it lively with a heavy dash of syncopation. Olee!

"La Paloma"

W/Spanish rhythm

Mix. D   (1st part)

Sebastian Yradier

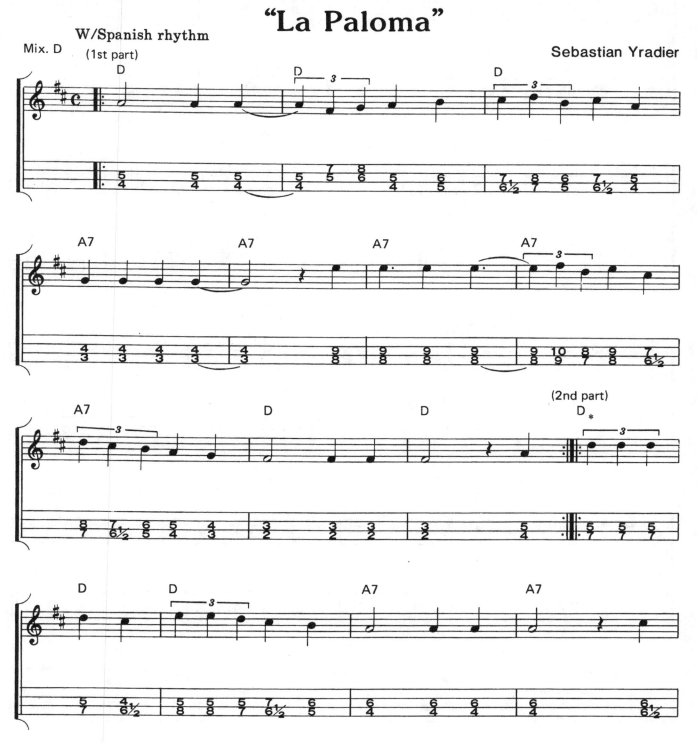

(‿ or ⌒) These are "Tiro" - They connect notes and are held for the total count of both added together.

* - Here we move from 3rds into 6ths - notice the distinct change in tone.

Photo by Mark Biggs

Written for my neice, Sonya Mun, this tune starts slow & builds steam clear to the end.
It moves along as sprightly as a happy young girl.

"Sonya's Song"

Mark Biggs

Dotted (𝅘𝅥.) notes receive half again as long a count as normal.

C (3rd part 1st phrase)

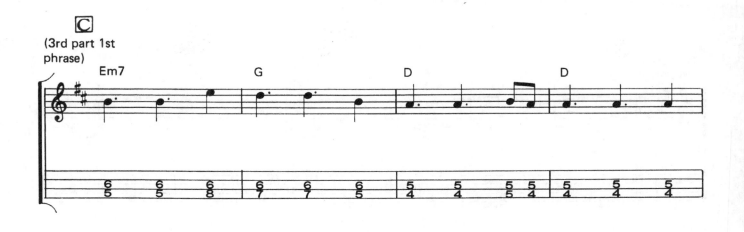

(2nd phrase)

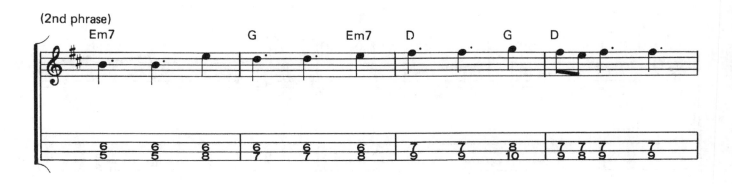

(3rd phrase)

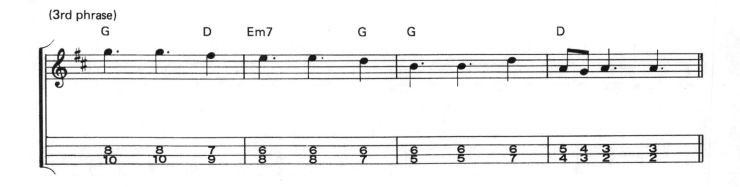

(2nd part) **B**

(2nd time through move into double time)

(2nd time through slow down to original tempo)

A

(1st part)
(1st phrase)

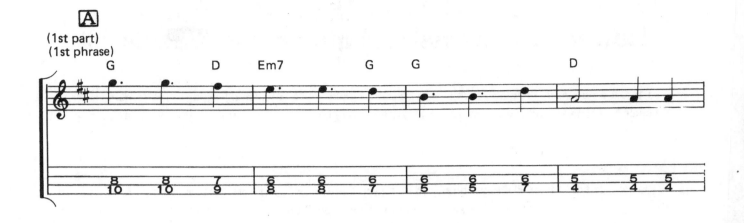

(2nd phrase)

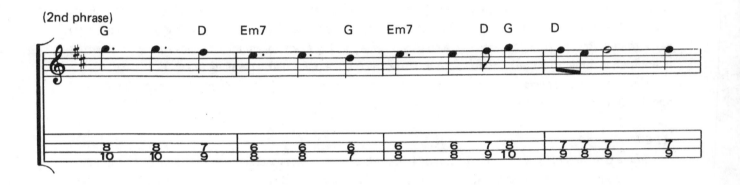

(3rd phrase)

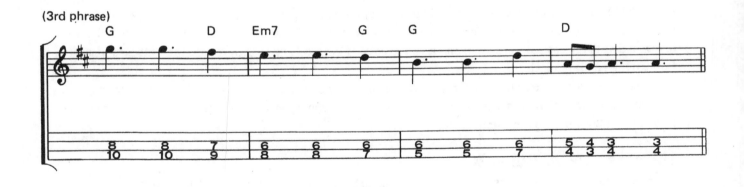

(2nd part)

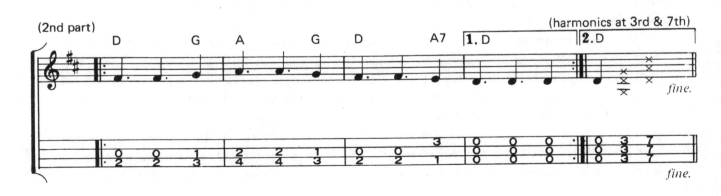

51

BASIC STRING TECHNIQUES:
Harmonics, Tremelo, Hammer-ons & Pull-offs

There are numerous techniques which can be used equally well on almost any stringed instrument. They add spice to a tune and offer yet another possibility for arranging a song. Here are three of these basic string techniques.

Harmonics

Harmonics are the bell-like tones produced when you lightly touch (just barely rest your finger on) the strings of your dulcimer, directly above one of the "nodes" positioned along the fretboard. A "node" is a point of natural division along the length of your string found at the 3rd, 4th, 7th, 11th, and 14th frets. When you barely rest the flat of your finger **directly above one of these frets,** then strike the strings you should hear a very soft clear tone. If you don't, lighten the pressure of your finger on the strings and try again. With practice you can open up the sound and volume of your harmonics by striking the strings and pulling your finger away just a fraction of a second later. You can also play a series of single note harmonics by moving from one string to another, leaping from one node to another. This can create a particularly pleasing effect.

Harmonics are especially nice at the beginnings and endings of songs; they give a distinct sense of opening or closure. I use them in this arranging style quite often.

Tremelo

Tremelo means to pick a string in a rapid backwards and forwards motion to create a sense of continual vibrating sound. This is the only way to sustain a note for a long period of time when using a flat pick—the only other way to sustain a note on a stringed instrument is to use a bow. Move into the tremelo slowly, starting with a back and forth picking motion across one string, gradually increasing speed until the pick's tip is literally riding the top of the string in a very rapid vibrating strum—the movement is from the wrist and tremor-like. When I use the tremelo technique I brace my ring finger (of the picking hand) against the side of the fretboard to give me a steady base to work from, and turn the edge of the pick's tip slightly toward the fretboard to cut through the string more cleanly.

Like harmonics, the tremelo technique works well as a way to begin or end a song. It sounds especially nice when used with slow passages, or as a way to spice up an unadorned melody line. Try tremeloing your way through "Oh Susanna" to see what I mean.

Hammer-ons & Pull-offs

These are two of the most useful and lovely string techniques on the mountain dulcimer, and are performed exactly as their names indicate. They can be used separately, or in conjunction with one another to create a most pleasant effect known in Elizabethan music as a "double mordant," which is a hammer-on followed by a pull-off, or vice-versa.

To create a hammer-on, pluck the string (either open or fretted at some chosen note) and immediately thereafter bring one of your free fingers down forcefully on a fret **up** the fretboard from the original note. You are actually using your finger as a hammer to sound out the second note. In the beginning your forefinger will probably work best; though in time it is possible to hammer-on two or even three notes in rapid succession to produce a kind of trilling effect. For practice, place your middle finger on the third fret of your melody string. Now strike the string with your pick and immediately hammer down on the fourth fret with your index finger. Try this from different positions, and even try fretting the dulcimer at the first fret with your ring finger before hammering down on the second and third frets in rapid succession with your middle and index fingers respectively.

When you perform a "pull-off" you are actually sounding or plucking the string with your noting hand. Unlike the hammer-on where you come straight down on the string from directly above it, with the pull-off you bring your "pulling" finger **up and off to the side, actually plucking the string as you leave it.** Just pluck the open melody string with your fretting hand's index finger for a moment to get the feel of this motion. Now put your middle finger on the third fret of the melody string, and your index finger on the fourth fret. From this position, without striking the string with your pick, pull your index finger back towards you and away from the melody string. This should sound the string with the same tone as if you had simply picked the string while holding the third fret down. If it doesn't, try again and remember to pull on the string as you lift away from it with your index finger. In essence you are finger-picking the string with your noting hand.

Finally, let's put the two techniques together. Again, fret the melody string at the third fret with your middle finger. Strike the string only once with your pick, then hammer down on the fourth fret with your index finger and immediately pull-off from the fourth fret with your index finger, keeping your middle finger on the third fret. This should give you a da-dum-da sound, which is the triplet stroke known as a "double mordant". If you run a series of double mordants down the melody string you get a most lovely sound, one particularly characteristic of the dulcimer. Hammer-ons and pull-offs are particularly useful when jamming with a friend, or improvising a lead line, or to accent a passage within a song.

BARRE CHORDING IN THE MIXOLYDIAN MODE

Without a doubt, the technique known as "barre chording" is one of the most useful things you can learn how to do on your dulcimer. It allows you to play in different keys out of one modal tuning without having to retune. It also enables you to move through a number of chord patterns which share one common fret point without having to move your hand from the initial barre chord position. The barre chord technique is quite difficult to develop however, so once again be patient with yourself as you work to gain control over it.

Since I never use my thumb when playing the dulcimer, I compensate for this absence by making extensive use of barre chords. They are in fact the secret which underlies many of my more advanced arrangements, and you will almost certainly find it necessary to conquer this string technique before you will be able to play these arrangements with ease. **Barre chords are formed when you "stop", or hold down, all three strings across one fret using only one finger to accomplish this task.** A guitarist uses his index finger to form barre chords because his hand is held behind the neck of his instrument. When playing the dulcimer however, your hand is positioned above the fretboard (as on a keyboard instrument) with your palm facing down, finger out and away from you. As a result, your little finger assumes the function of barre chording. This creates special problems since your pinky is probably your weakest finger. I remember that when I first began to barre chord with my little finger it was both difficult and painful; my finger seemed to possess a will of its own, deciding where and when to go of its own accord, stinging from the strings which cut into it, and complaining about the cramp paralyzing the outside muscle of my hand. Familiar stories to anyone who has ever learned how to barre chord a stringed instrument. In time, with practice, you will gain control, subtlety, strength and quickness with your little finger—a callous will develop to protect your tender digit, and you will undoubtedly sport the hottest adductor muscle on your block. And most importantly, your dulcimer playing will have significantly improved.

Even if you use your thumb when playing, the ability to form barre chords will prove valuable in a number of dramatic ways.

Being able to barre chord with your little finger provides you with a built-in capo which allows you to change keys without retuning. Barring at the correct fret in effect "retunes" the dulcimer for you. In the Mixolydian Mode, key of D, you can produce these capoed keys:

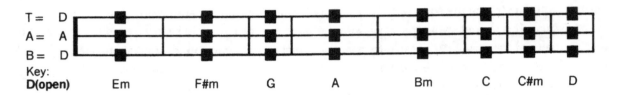

If you have a mechanical capo (one built for the guitar or specifically for the dulcimer), it can be used in the same manner to change the key you are playing in. Even a pencil and rubber band can be turned into a mechanical capo. However if you learn to use your little finger you can do things like changing keys in the middle of a song—an arranging technique which is sometimes quite dramatic. Remember that if you do use the barre chord to change keys, you must still play the correct notes found in the scale of that key. We'll look at the A & G-scales played out of the D Mixolydian tuning in Finger Exercise #3. (To figure out what notes would be found in a major scale, review the appendix section on Major and Minor scales.)

I want you to be aware that it is possible and sometimes advantageous to bar with your third or ring finger instead of with the little finger. I often use the third finger when barre chording high up on the fretboard (in the 8,9,10th fret range), simply because its' easier and gives me a cleaner sound.

More important (and perhaps less confusing) than this capoing use of the barre chord, is the opportunity it affords you to pass quickly and easily through a large number of chord forms. With your little finger in the barre position you can slide from one chord into another sharing one or more notes on the common bottom fret. For instance, starting in the Mixolydian key of D from a G chord position, we can move through the following chords:

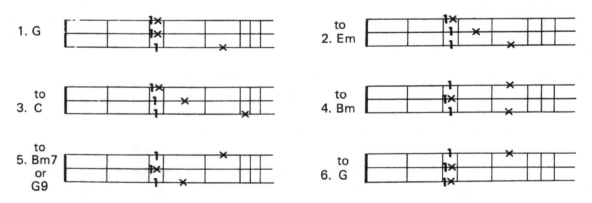

The barre chord position also allows us to invert certain chord forms quickly and easily. One chord form, the L form such as the G chord used above, is particularly useful in this context, though the other two major chord forms can also be inverted from the barre chord base. The inversions look like:

G chord:

D chord:

C chord:

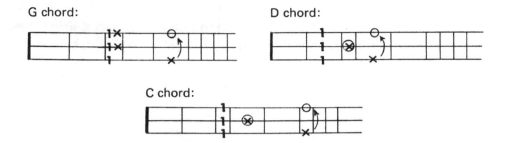

One last word before we look at a couple of songs, I very frequently will keep my little finger in the bar position even if the chord I'm playing doesn't require me to do so. For instance I'll often play a slant form G chord (with the melody note on the 7th fret) with my little finger barred across the 5th fret. I do this so that I can move into other chord positions rapidly, or because the melody line note will drop below the 7th fret yet still remains backed by a G chord. Some simple experimenting on your part should quickly tell you whether or not this underpinning barre position will prove helpful.

Try the barre chord with the next song, "Jacky Tar", and old sea chantey in the key of Em played out of the D - Mixolydian tuning.

"Jacky Tar" is a hornpipe, and so should go moderately fast. From the feel of it, I think it's probably English in origin, which is where some musical scholars believe the ancient double-reed instrument called a "hornpipe" originated. Hornpipes later became dances and began to be particularly associated with seamen in the 18th Century, perhaps as part of the compulsary exercise these seamen had to under go. So move lightly with this beautiful tune, limber up slowly and then dance the tar out of this song.

"Jacky Tar"

Hornpipe

RHYTHM EXERCISE #3: 3/4 Rhythm Practice

So far we have dealt exclusively with songs written in 4/4 (four-four) time. As mentioned earlier there are many different time signatures, each one of which lends a song a completely different rhythm and feeling. In this book we will work with the more common signatures of: 3/4, 4/4, 6/8, and perhaps 6/4. The time signature appears immediately after the bar clef (which tells us what octave range the song is written in) and the appropriate #'s and b's which tell us what key the song is written in. Essentially the time signature tells us how many beats per measure we have, and clues us in to the rhythm of the piece. (See the appendix on READING TIME VALUES for details.)

For now let's skip most of the theory and look directly at our second time signature, 3/4 time. After you have worked with a few different time signatures, just seeing them at the head of a new song will give you some idea of the tempo (how fast to play the piece) and mood of the song. 4/4 time usually signifies a straight ahead approach; it is the common signature of marches, country dance tunes, reels & hornpipes, as well as the wealth of tunes we hear daily on the radio. 3/4 time has traditionally been played slower, and more stately than 4/4 time; 3/4 is the common signature of waltzes & minuets, as well as a great many Irish airs and a fair number of Renaissance dance tunes. We are going to work with the 3/4 signature now as we go through our standard rhythm exercise one last time. We will use three different chords this time, chosen from the L-shaped chord form:

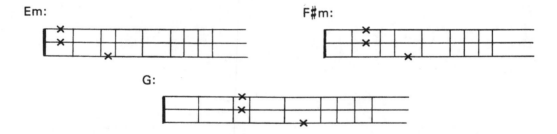

Once again our basic picking pattern will start: all away, then all towards us, then away and towards, move into double time (both directions twice as fast), then drop back into the original time strumming both directions, then all towards us, and end with the strokes going all away from us. This time the count will be: 1, 2, 3/ 1, 2, 3/ 1, 2, 3/ etc., so get your foot tapping and count out loud. You can alternate strokes evenly all the way through the appropriate points in this exercise exactly as you did in the 4/4 exercise, or you can strum away on the 1st count, towards you on the 2nd, and away on the 3rd count for each measure. Graphically this second picking pattern looks like this:

```
1  2  3  /  1  2  3  / etc.
↑  ↓  ↑     ↑  ↓  ↑
```

Sometimes strumming like this helps keep tract of the 3/4 rhythm and prevents you from unconsciously slipping back into 4/4. Another way to avoid jumping from 3/4 into 4/4 is to "accent" the first beat of every 3/4 measure -- simply strumming a bit harder on the first count to accentuate that beat.

Let's begin the exercise with the Em(L-form) chord and side straight up and down the fretboard through the F#m and G chords, switching the chord form everytime you change picking direction.

Follow the pattern: (In. = inverted form as shown in the last section.)

Em   F#m   G   In.G   In.F#m   In.Em   Em

Practice this 3/4 rhythm exercise with these chords and the D and Em slant chord forms we used in the last rhythm section until you have a firm feel for the 3/4 time signature and are able to smoothly invert the new L-shaped chord form. Notice that this Mixolydian chord form is built around the barre chord technique, so work this exercise into your daily warm-ups as a way to slowly increase your barre chording ability. Before moving on, here are four songs which should help get you started playing in 3/4 time. The first song, "Silent Night," is also an excellent song to practice your set-chording techniques on. I often play "When Johnny Comes Marching Home" and "The Road to Lisdoonvarna" together as a medley since their two melody lines work so well together.

"Silent Night"

Trad. Christmas Hymn

"Sweet Betsy from Pike"

* Triplet with last two notes being optional ''grace notes'' created by a hammer-on & pull-off.

Sweet Betsy From Pike

Did you ever hear tell of Sweet Betsy from Pike,
She cross the whole country with her old husband Ike,
With two yoke of oxen and one spotted hog,
A tall Shanghai rooster, and an ole yeller dog.

Chorus:
Singing too-rall-i-oo-rall-i-oo-rall-i-aye.
Singing too-rall-i-oo-rall-i-oo-rall-i-aye.

Well one evening quite early they camped by the Platt,
T'was nearby the river on a green shady flat.
Now Betsy quite tired lay down to repose,
While with wonder Ike gazed on his Pike County rose.

At last one fine morning they climbed a tall hill,
And in wonder, gazed down upon old Placerville.
Ike raved and he ranted as he cast his eyes down,
"Sweet Betsy, my darling, there lies old Hangtown."

Sweet Betsy and Ike, they got married of course.
But Ike getting ansy, obtained a divorce.
And Betsy well satisfied said with a shout,
"Goodbye you big lummox, I'm glad you backed out."

"When Johnny Comes Marching Home"

When Johnny Comes Marching Home

When Johnny comes marching home again,
    Hurray, Hurray.
We'll give him a hearty welcome then,
    Hurroo, Hurroo.
Oh the men will shout, and the boys will cheer,
The ladies they will all turn out,
And we'll all feel gay when
Johnny come marching home.

The old church bell will peal with joy
    Hurray, Hurray.
To welcome home our hearty boys,
    Hurroo, Hurroo.
The village lads and lassies say,
With roses they will strew the was,
And we'll all feel gay when
Johnny comes marching home.

Johnny I Hardly Knew You

Johnny I hardly knew you
   with your guns & drums, & drums & guns,
   Hurray, Hurray.
With your guns & drums, & drums & guns
   Hurroo, Hurroo.
With your guns & drums, & drums & guns,
The enemy nearly slew you.
Oh, my darling dear, you look so queer,
Oh Johnny I hardly knew you.

Where are your legs that used to run,
   Hurrah, Hurrah.
Where are your legs that used to run,
   Hurroo, Hurroo.
Oh, where are your legs that used to run
When first you went to carry a gun,
Yes, my darling dear, you look so queer,
Oh Johnny I hardly knew you.

They're rolling out the drums again,
   Hurrah, Hurrah.
They're rolling out the drums again,
   Hurroo, Hurroo.
Yes, they're rolling out the drums again,
But they'll never take our sons again,
No, they'll never take our sons again,
Oh, Johnny I'm swearing to you.

"The Road to Lisdoonvarna"

Trad. Irish

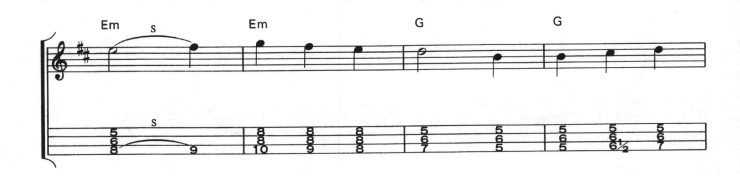

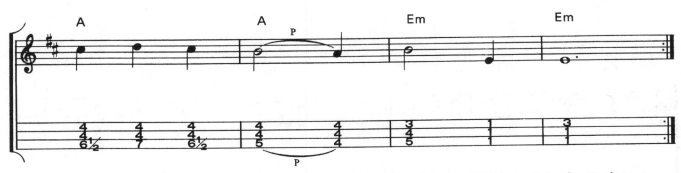

* "Road To Lisdoonvarna" is in fact an Irish jig, written in 6/8 rather than 3/4 time. It is often easier to drop a new song from the faster paced 6/8 into 3/4 when learning the song. Later as you speed the song up, you'll move back into 6/8 - everything stays the same, you simply squeeze 2 bars into one measure. In 6/8 the song looks like this:

The Road to Lisdoonvarna
(in 6/8)

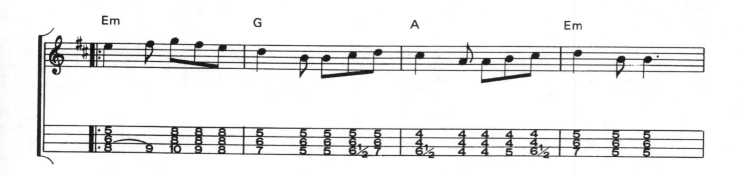

Photo by Mark Biggs

THE THREE BASIC CHORD FORMS:
In the Mixolydian Mode

There are three basic, or root chord forms in the Mixolydian Mode. We have already worked with two of them: the slant (/) chord form used in the 2nd Rhythm Exercise (D and Em), and the L-chord form used in the 3rd Rhythm Exercise. We will deal with the third form, the double-slant (or its abbreviated T form) below. All fretted string instruments have basic chord patterns which can be moved along the fretboard to create new chords built on the same form. This means that you can commit the name of one chord in one form to memory, and then be able to figure out the name of an unknown chord based on this same chord form at any other point on your dulcimer. You can do this by learning the basic chord pattern which runs up the dulcimer's fretboard. Don't begin to groan now. If this doesn't make sense at present it will in a moment with the aid of diagrams.

In effect, we have three basic chord forms and one preestablished chord progression pattern. **This means that once we know the unalterable chord progression, and have memorized the name of one chord in each of the three chord forms, we can determine the name of any unknown chord which is based on one of these three fundamental forms.** Instead of memorizing 25 chords in a random way (not an easy task, let me assure you), we have to memorize only 3 chords (carefully chosen) and the fixed chord progression which runs up and down the dulcimer's fretboard.

First let's review the three basic chord forms. If you prefer to memorize different ones that is fine. Remember we are tuned in the key of D, Mixolydian Mode so we have the open notes of DD A D on our strings. The chord names will change depending on the key you are in, but the forms will remain constant.

1.) The slant (\ ) form:
   D chord

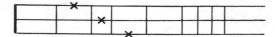

The slant chord form takes its chord name from the note found on the middle string. Here

the note on the third fret of the middle string is D, so we have a D chord. You must still remember

the major/ minor chord progression which runs up the dulcimer's fretboard (see below), but knowing

which string gives the chord form its name should prove useful.

2.) The L- form:
   Em chord

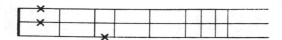

The L-form chord derives its name from the bass string note; here the note is E so we have an

Em chord. Recognize that if you use an inverted form, the name of the chord would be found on

the melody string.

3.) The double-slant (＼) form:

Bm chord

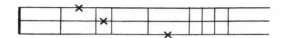

    The note found on the melody string gives us the name of the double-slant chord form. If the chord is played in its inverted position, the bass string becomes the naming note.

    Note: This chord can also be played in the T-form which is far easier to finger, but prevents you from inverting the chord. It is built on the split-octave chord.

T-form: Bm chord

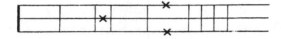

(Here both melody and bass strings lend the chord its name.)

Once we have memorized one chord in each of the three basic forms, we must then turn to the chord progression pattern which runs like this:

Key of D:
          D, Em, F♯m, G, A, Bm, C (or A7 in ＼ form), D

(or key of E:)
          E, F♯m, G♯m, A, B, C♯m, D (or B7 in ＼ form), E

(or key of F:)
          F, Gm, Am, B, C, Dm, E (or C7 in ＼ form), F

(or key of G:)
          G, Am, Bm, C, D, Em, F (or D7 in ＼ form), G

(or key of A:)
          A, Bm, C♯m, D, E, F♯m, G (or E7 in ＼ form), A

(or key of B:)
          B, C♯m, D♯m, E, F, G♯m, A (or F♯7 in ＼ form), B

(or key of C:)
          C, Dm, Em, F, G, Am, B (or G7 in ＼ form), C

In the Mixolydian Mode the chord progression always runs through the series:

Major, minor, minor, major, major, minor, major (or 7th), major
(D)   (D one octave higher)

    In other words, running our chord pattern up the fretboard, we always move through this major-minor progression: (Read symbols from right to left.)

1.) Slant (\ ) form: (D D   A   D Tuning)

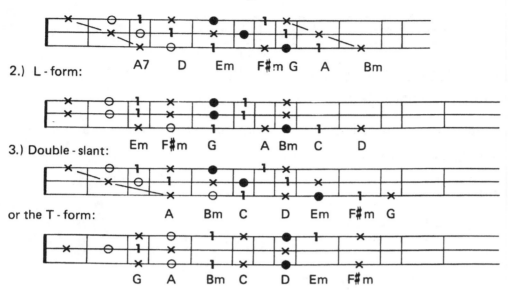

A7   D   Em   F♯m G   A   Bm

2.) L - form:

Em F♯m   G   A Bm   C   D

3.) Double - slant:

A   Bm   C   D   Em   F♯m G

or the T - form:

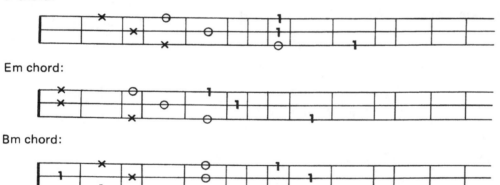

G   A   Bm   C   D   Em   F♯m

Slide up and down through these three forms and see if you can't begin to hear the same chords being repeated in different positions along the fretboard. When you are comfortable with there three forms and the standard chord progression, try to begin to associate the same chord in its three different positions along the fretboard. For instance:

D chord:

Em chord:

Bm chord:

As you begin to make these associations you'll move well down the road towards the goal of being able to put the chord structure of a song behind its melody line. For once you know the three positions of the chord (along with the possible inversions), you should be able to figure out which chord form will fit most easily behind each melody note.

ARRANGING A SONG:
Putting the Chord Structure Behind the Melody.

From the start of this book, you have been learning how to accomplish this fundamental arranging technique. Everything we have studied so far has prepared you to move easily into this style of playing. The first step, as always, is to learn the melody line of the song you wish to put the chord structure behind. Once you know the melody, you will have an idea of how the song takes you along the fretboard. This is crucial, for until you know this pattern of movement you can't begin to decide what chord form you'll want to use in conjunction with each melody note. When you are comfortable with the melody line, look at the chords written above it and refer to the dulcimer chord charts in the back of this book (or to your memory banks where the chord forms are stored). Finally; you can begin to decide which fingers to use to play the chord structure together with the melody note. Most of the time you can keep the melody note on the melody string and use the middle and bass strings to play the supporting chord structure. As you decide which fingers to use, and what frets to note on which strings, you should write the slowly emerging arrangement down in dulcimer tablature so you can refer to it later.

Here are the first four bars of the "Minuet in G" by Bach, laid out to show you how this method proceeds:

"Minuet in G"

J. S. Bach

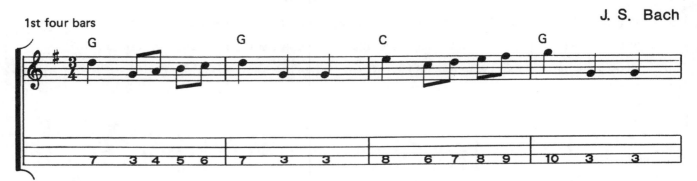

Having played throught this melody line a couple of times, look up (or recall) the chord froms for G and C. They look like this:

G chords:

C chords:

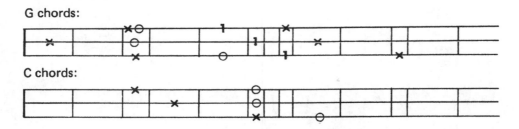

(Always remember that you can invert a chord in the Mixolydian Mode.) Once you have a handle on the melody line and the potential chord forms, begin to cross-check between the two, carefully choosing your chords as you work through the piece note by note. Since the opening note is a D at the 7th fret we choose the G slant chord form:

G chord:

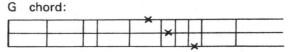

Finding the next note at the third fret and looking ahead two or three notes, we choose to move next into the barre chord L-form of G, which will most easily enable us to play the next sequence of notes. So we use this G form:

G chord L - form:

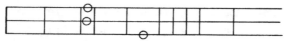

We slide through the C note at the 6th fret, as we return to grab the original G slant chord form, just before falling back into the L-form G chord. Now the chord structure changes to C, so we review the C chord options and select the L-form C chord which (like the L-form G chord) allows us to play a series of melody notes from the barre chord position. This C chord looks like:

C chord L - form:

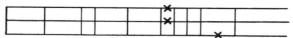

Clearly, a different C chord form would not be as well suited. Likewise when we move to the G note at the 10th fret, a G chord other than the double-slant form would not work as well, Here's how the song looks with the full tab written out:

Minuet in G

Mixolydian D
(DD A D)
Key of G

A classic 17th century dance from one of the baroque masters. Baroque music is exceptionally well suited to the dulcimer because of its frequent use of modes and modal scales. I occasionally like to slip into 4/4 time to give the song some swing (this can easily be done by extending the 1st note of the measure by 1 beat.)

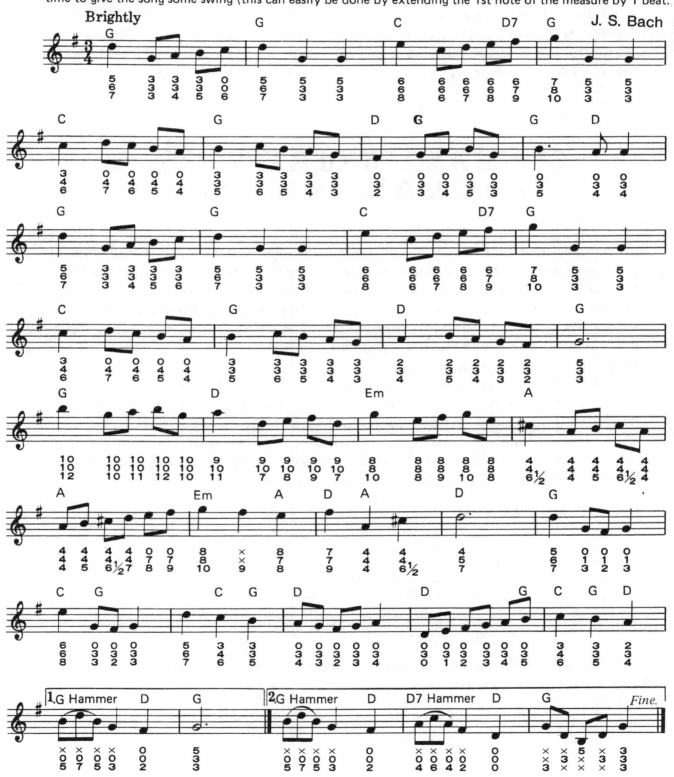

73

This procedure of placing the chord structure behind the melody line is clearly a step by step process of foresight and compromise. You not only have to locate the chord form you need, but you also have to make sure you'll be able to play the required fingering later on. Some fingering patterns will clearly prove too difficult, so you'll have to compromise on a partial chord, or fall back into an unadorned melody line to get through these difficult passages. Recognize your limitations, but don't be afraid to try new or difficult fingerings. Remember you can always play two finger partial chords until you feel ready to move on to full three finger chords. You'll soon discover what works best for yourself. The idea behind this arranging technique is to create a pleasurable challenge for yourself, and simultaneously to make your dulcimer playing sound more full and rich. Give the technique a chance before writing it off as too difficult; you might just surprise yourself.

SCALE AND FINGER EXERCISE #3:
The G & A Scales in a D Tuning

Previously we mentioned the possibility of playing in different keys out of one modal tuning without having to retune our dulcimers. We've seen how the barre chord can be used to help accomplish this important technique. Let's look now at the second component you must study before you can change keys at will. You must learn what notes are in the key you wish to play in so that you can hit only those notes as you move up and down the fretboard. In effect, if you play a series of notes not included in a key, you will not be playing in that key. Again I refer you to the appendix on major and minor keys to review the basic formula for determining what notes occur in any certain key.

In the first finger exercise we learned the D scale, as played from a D tuning in the Mixolydian Mode. In this second finger exercise we are going to study the <u>G scale</u> as played again in the D tuning (Mixolydian Mode). The finger patterns we'll follow will correspond to those used to play the original D-scale-- only the starting position changes. Instead of beginning from the open string position, we'll start this time on the third fret. Follow the numbers up the fretboard in the first diagram, then reverse and come back down exactly as you went up.

G scale: (D tuning, Mix. Mode)

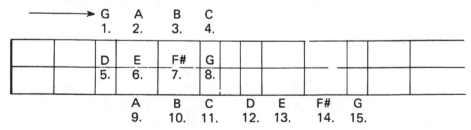

Now walk up and across the fretboard as you just did, but come back down by following the diagram below which shows you some alternative "cross-over" points:

G scale:

				G 15.	A 14.		B 13.	C 12.		D 11.	E 10.				

(fretboard diagram)

Middle row:
9 F# | 8 G | 7 A | 6 B

Bottom row:
5. C | 4. D | 3. E | 2. F# | 1. G ←———————

Practice these G scales until you feel comfortable with them. Listen carefully (as always) to the sound of the G scale and try to hear the differences between it and the D scale. They are sympathetic keys so the difference, while not great, will still be distinct.

Let's also work with the A scale as played out of the D tuning. If we study the formula for determining what notes fall in what scales, we discover that the key of D has two sharps (C#, & F#); the key of G has only one sharp (F#); and the key of A has three sharps (C#, F#, & G#). We are able to play the G scale easily because the key of D has two sharps, one of which is shared by the key of G. The A scale includes a G# note however, so we will be somewhat restricted when playing the key of A out of our D tuning. Armed with the 6 1/2 fret however, we can play one full octave of the A scale. It looks like this:

A scale: (out of the D duning, Mix. Mode)

A 1. | B 2. | | C# 3. | D 4. | | | | | | |

(fretboard diagram)

Middle/bottom:
E 5. | F# 6. | | G# 7. | A 8.

By arranging a song in the key of A so that we are near the middle string's 6 1/2 fret when we need a G# note, we can play in this key with relatively few difficulties. Below are several songs which are played in the keys of G and A out of the Mixolydian D tuning.

Before we look at them I want you to understand that in the Mixolydian Mode we can always play the key we are tuned in, plus its relative minor, plus the fourth (4th) and the fifth (5th) keys along with their relative minor keys.

Open Key	Relative minor	4th	Rel. Minor	5th	Rel. Minor
D (DD A D)	Bm	G	Em	A	F#m
C (CC G C)	Am	F	Dm	G	Em
E (EE B E)	C#m	A	F#m	B	G#m

"Oh Susanna"
(in the Key of G)

This is one of my favorite Stephen Foster songs. I fear its theme will remain forever part of mankind's lot, but the feelings which Foster captures so poignantly in "Hard Times" make this a unique contribution in the unending campaign to help ease suffering. It speaks to me as surely as it spoke to the Okies headed west in the 1930s, and to the poor rural folk of post–Civil War America. But then Stephen Foster himself knew a little bit about hard times, for despite his many famous melodies he died alone and in poverty in New York's Bellevue Hospital in 1864, the same year "Beautiful Dreamer" was published.

"Hard Times Come Again No More"

Stephen Foster

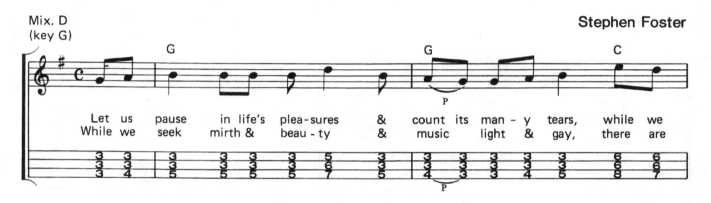

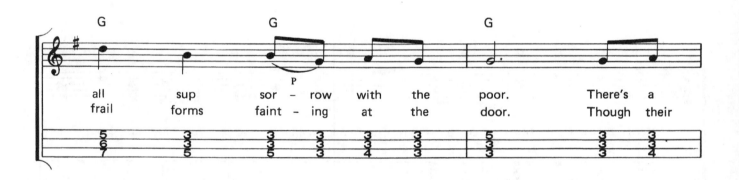

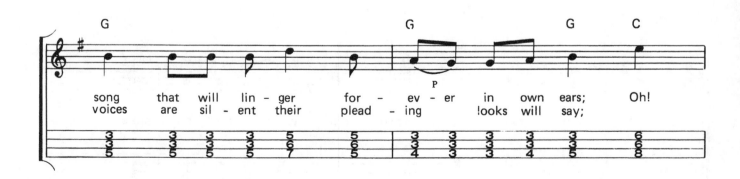

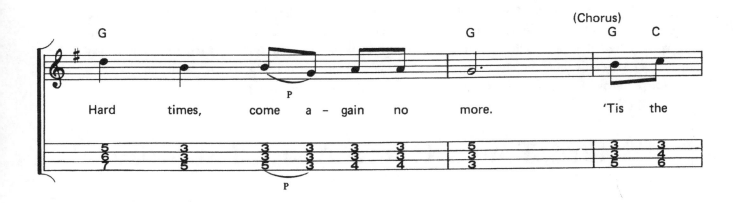

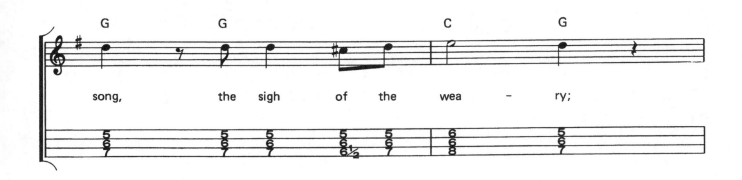

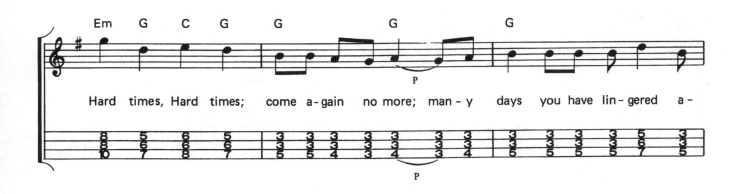

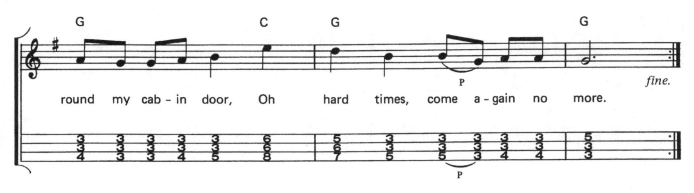

78

Hard Times Come Again No More

Let us pause in life's pleasures
    And count its many tears,
While we all sup sorrow with the poor;
There's a song that will linger
    Forever in our ears;
Oh! Hard Times, come again no more.

Chorus:
    Tis the song, the sigh of the weary;
    Hard Times, Hard Times, come again no more;
    Many days you have lingered around my cabin door,
    Oh! Hard Times, come again no more.

While we seek mirth and beauty
    And music light and gay,
There are frail forms fainting at the door;
Though their voices are silent,
    Their pleading looks will say,
Oh! Hard Times, come again no more.

"My Old Kentucky Home, Good Night"

"Red River Valley"

Mix. D
(key of A)

Trad. Am. Folksong

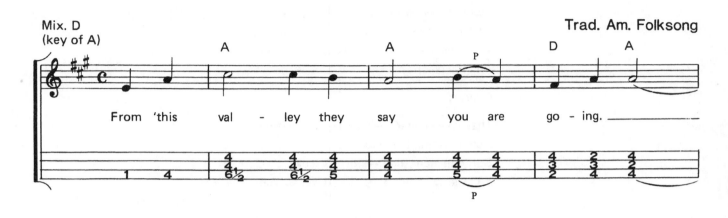

From 'this val – ley they say you are go – ing. _____

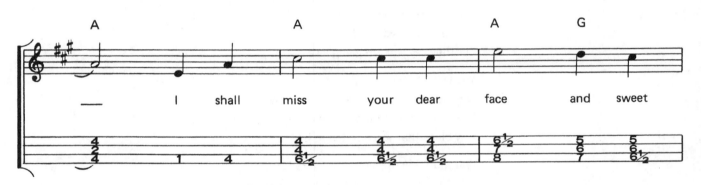

_____ I shall miss your dear face and sweet

smile. When you leave you will take all the

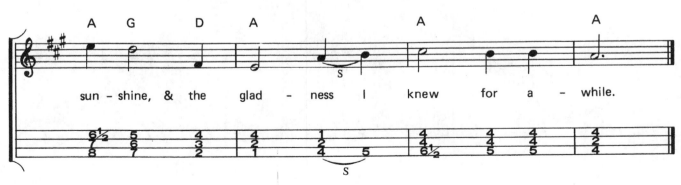

sun – shine, & the glad – ness I knew for a – while.

Red River Valley

From this valley they say you are going,
I will miss your dear face and sweet smile,
When you leave you will take all the sunshine,
And the gladness I knew for a while.

Chorus:

Then come linger a while e'er you leave me,
Do not hasten to bid me adieu,
But remember the Red River Valley,
And the sweetheart that loved you so true.

I have listened a long time my darling,
For the words that you never would say,
Now at last must my dreams all be shattered,
For they say you are going away.

You will never be happy with strangers,
For they don't understand you like we,
But you'll know that our prayers will be with you,
Any place that you happen to be.

Will you think of the valley you're leaving,
And the old folks whose thoughts are of you?
Will you think of the hearts you have broken,
And the sweetheart who loved you so true?

Here's red hot little number for you. Another hornpipe, this time from Ireland where it was originally called "An Giolla Ruadh" (an geely rooach). And a peck of 'rooach's' has always been cause to get up and dance in my humble opinion. Play it fast with plenty of lilt and a wee bit of Irish brogue.

"Red Haired Boy"

83

The "Arkansas Traveller", one of the most popular American fiddle tunes, came out of a hit play produced in Ohio in 1850. The play concerned an Arkansas fiddler's attempts to recall the ending of a tune he'd heard in New Orleans. Such are the subjects of great literature-- nonetheless this is a great tune. Play it moderately fast and take special notice of the point when the song leaves the key of A behind and goes merrily on into the key of D. (A flat-picked version is presented in a few pages.)

"Arkansas Traveller"

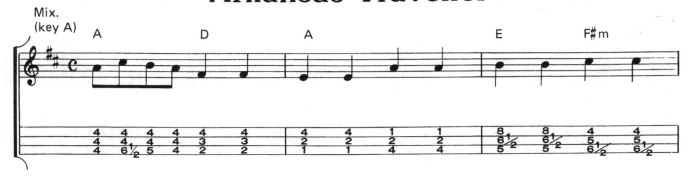

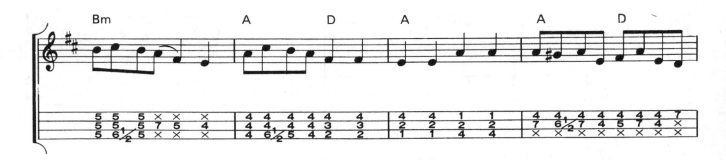

* Here we start in the key of A & switch into the key of D.

(Key of D)

86

FLAT-PICKING:
A Way to Play Melody Lines On Single Strings

While we are at this juncture, let's use two of these fine old traditional tunes to illustrate a basic picking technique called **flat-picking**. Quite simply, this technique uses the flat-pick to rapidly pick out the melody line of a song across all three strings of your dulcimer. Though it is certainly more difficult to put into practice than it sounds, flat-picking is often an excellent way to vary an arrangement of a familiar song. When flat-picking you should pay particular attention to the direction you will pick a certain note; usually you will alternate each stroke, picking away then towards yourself. Sometimes when playing fast, you may find it necessary to give each note a double stroke (pick away and towards quickly) in order to keep the flow of the music moving smoothly. In a sense you are simply falling into double time when you use this "double stroke".

Here are "The Arkansas Traveller" and the "Red Haired Boy" written in flat-pick tab with direction arrows to show you the picking direction of each note in the melody line.

Photo by Mark Biggs

87

"The Red Haired Boy"
(Flat-Picked Version)

* I've written this 8va, or one octave above where the notes would actually fall, to make it easier to sight - read.

"Arkansas Traveller"
(Flatpick Version)

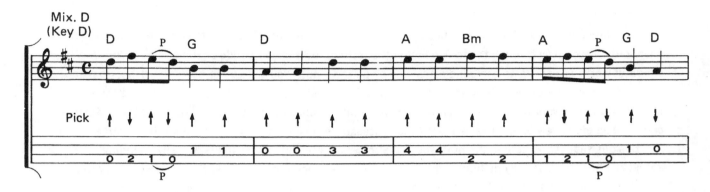

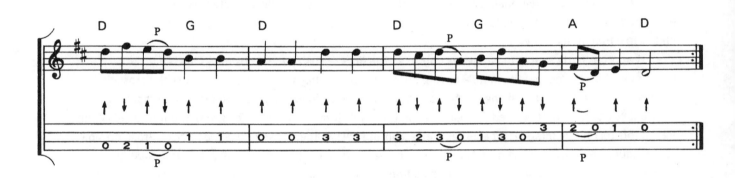

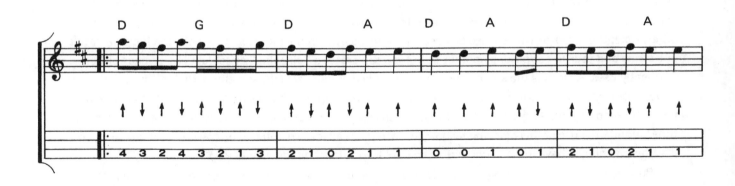

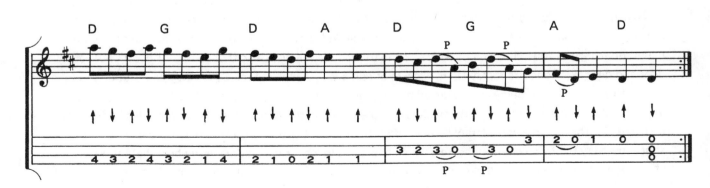

BASIC STRING TECHNIQUES #2:
Slides, Bends, Finger-brush & Bowing

Here are a few more string techniques which you can use to arrange, or simply to add a touch of color to your songs as you play through them. The first of the techniques is called a **slide** or sometimes a **slur**. Very simply, it works exactly as its name indicates: having picked a note, you slide up or down the string from one note to another without ever lifting your finger. You do this rapidly so that the slide rings out while the string is still vibrating from your initial strum. Many Irish and Scottish songs call for slurs or slides, and the technique can be used effectively to emphasize a particular passage within a tune. Give it a try; it's actually quite simple.

Besides sliding one note to the next, you can also **bend** a note. In effect you are actually "bending" the sound of a note by physically pulling on the string after it has been noted and struck with the pick. Try this now. Fret the middle string at the third fret, pick the string and pull it towards you slowly. Hear the sound bend? You can get a wah-wah sound by bending the note (pulling the string towards you, and pushing it back to the original position then pulling it again—try this rather rapidly.) Bending a note gives you a nice "bluesy" effect and can sometimes provide just the right touch—it can sound like a human cry, or summon a smile if placed in a humorous context.

Yet another fairly simple technique is known as the **finger-brush** (at least by me). This is a picking technique whereby you use the middle or ring finger of your picking-strumming hand to brush across the strings. Brushing across the strings with the fleshy part of your finger tip gives the dulcimer a distinctly different sound from that created by your pick; on the whole it mutes the strings, giving them a harp-like tone. Again, this technique offers great arranging or accenting possibilities. I like to use it as a backstroke on slow songs, especially with old Irish harp tunes where it seems to make the dulcimer sing soft and sweetly. Generally I'll stroke more slowly with my middle finger as I brush back across the strings. This accentuates the harp-like effect and produces a kind of **glissando** or arpeggiated sound as if you were brushing across the strings of a harp. (A glissando is created by gliding the back of your finger over a keyboard or across the strings of a harp, while an arpeggio is a chord broken into its separate notes which are played one directly after the other.) **Note:** the finger-brush can also be used simultaneously with the pick. Together between the pick hitting one string and your finger picking another string you can create a "pinching" effect just like a finger picker frequently uses. A **pinch** is the simultaneous picking of two or more strings, something that is physically impossible using only a flatpick. This pinching technique will require a bit of concentration and some practice, but it will soon be quite easy and will enable you to play some unusual harmony notes. Many Renaissance tunes require the use of this pinching technique since they call for two notes to be played simultaneously, so it's a handy thing to have in your repetoire. (See the "Handsome Couple", page 121.)

Bowing is another tool you might consider bringing into your catalogue of string effects. I've had great success with it for about two years now and can vouch for its immediate spellbinding affect on an audience. The bow lends a haunting, sometimes melancholy, sometimes spine-tingling quality to the mountain dulcimer. It is much more difficult to gain a control over than the techniques described above, yet ultimately it offers a much greater reward. However, I advise you to find a secluded spot to begin bowing your dulcimer since the usual squaking and squealing sounds you're bound to produce will please neither your poor pooch, nor your near and dear loved ones. In fact, you are likely to offend even yourself at first. So once again I caution you to bare with yourself and to persevere. I started bowing the dulcimer on a whim just before I cut my first album, and only later discovered that the original dulcimer players up in the Appalachian Mountains also bowed their instruments. Theirs was a considerably cruder affair than the 3/4 size violin bow I presently use. It was a short bow, very tightly strung with horse or mule hair so as to form a deep curve in the bow shaft. It was strung this way because instead of coming over the top of the fretboard as I do, their bow shaft was positioned underneath the instrument allowing the bow hair to fall across all three or four strings of the dulcimer, once again providing that continual droning sound which the hill folk prized so highly. I prefer a somewhat less "hurdy-gurdy" or "portive chord-organ" sound (two medieval instruments which produce a droning sound similar to the bowed dulcimer), so I attack the strings from above. With the bow shaft located over the fretboard near the bridge I can hit either the melody or bass string separately, or draw across all three strings to produce a full chord effect. This gives me the option of playing a single note melody line or of playing the melody with the chord structure behind it.

I remain seated when I bow the dulcimer, which means a good share of the bowing motion and control comes from my wrist. Unlike the strum, when you bow you must arch your wrist greatly, moving it up and down through its full range. You must also use exaggerated arm movements from the shoulder in order to draw the bow fully across the strings. This posture is sometimes rather awkward and may be partly responsible for any difficulty you'll face when you first begin to bow the dulcimer. Feel free to try other postures to see if they work better for you.

I hold the bow either just above the frog where the bow shaft is wrapped, or at the frog (the little piece of wood or plastic which allows you to tighten or loosen the tension of the bow hair.) This offers the best balance, and in bowing balance counts for everything. I use a 3/4 size child's bow that is well balanced and allows me to utilize its full length without cramping my shoulder. Because it's lighter and shorter I'm quicker with it and can exert a much greater degree of control over my "vibrato" stroke (a very rapid backwards and forwards sawing motion which creates a tremelo effect with the bow—again a kind of controlled tremor, this time from the whole arm and wrist). The wonderful thing about bowing, outside of the most unusual and pleasant sounds it draws forth from the dulcimer, is its ability to sustain a note almost indefinitely. When you strike a string it vibrates rapidly; at first rising above the desired pitch, then quickly settling back into the desired tone and gradually decaying towards silence. Quite the opposite, the bow produces a fairly flat (or steady) tone which may be sustained by "sawing" back and forth across the strings. This sustaining ability is sometimes a very useful, and quite dramatic arranging tool.

I particularly like to record the dulcimer with both a picked and a bowed version being blended together. This blend can be heard on my second album, SEASON OF THE DREAM, available nationwide on the Kicking Mule Record label (KM-221). The picked dulcimer fills the melodic and rhythmic needs, while the bowed dulcimer reinforces the melody and lends a warm continuo presence much like a cello or viola behind the picked dulcimer. If you make music with another dulcimer player (which you should do as often as possible), try playing a song which you both know, with one of you bowing the melody line (on either the melody or bass string) while the other person picks the tune just like always. I think you will both be duly impressed. Let me suggest you borrow a bow first before running out to buy one; then when you know you want to bow your dulcimer, purchase a reasonably decent bow in the $40 to $50 range. A cheap bow will create more problems than the meager savings will ever be worth.

Holding Bow

Proper Bowing Posture

CROSSPICKING:
A Basic Flat-Picking Technique

Before moving on to our third lesson, let's look at another picking technique, one which could well have a profound influence on your playing style when you get a grip on it. Used in conjunction with a straight strum, **crosspicking** can help solo performers sound as if they are simultaneously playing rhythm and lead mountain dulcimer.

Essentially, **crosspicking is a flat-picked style where you strike each individual string in a rapid pattern instead of strumming straight across all the strings.** As you pick through a crosspicking pattern you usually keep the melody line on the melody string and crosspick the chorded or open middle and bass strings to produce an arpeggiated or broken-chord effect. Crosspicking demands a much greater degree of control over the pick than strumming does. One way to develop this flatpick control is to begin by working with some easy crosspicking patterns. Before we jump into those patterns however, let me say that I often use my ringfinger as a pivot point, wedging it against the top of the dulcimer and the fretboard around the 10 fret when I crosspick. This provides a stable point from which to launch and control my crosspicking. See if this works for you as well.

As we said above, crosspicking means we break our straight-ahead strum down into single string picking patterns. To get started let's work with one basic pattern from which you can eventually branch out to play many different licks. **Note:** the only way to learn a pattern is to repeat it endlessly, so fit each pattern into a song you already know and just crosspick it to death.

The Basic Crosspicking Pattern:

1.) away from you on the melody string

2.) towards you on the bass string

3.) towards you on the middle string

(repeat the pattern over and over)

Graphically it looks like this: (numbers set the order, while the arrows show the picking direction.

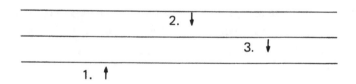

Sometimes I count this as a triplet (1 & a; 2 & a; 3 & a; 4 & a; etc., where the second stroke on the bass string = &, and the third stroke on the middle = a). If we put this crosspicking pattern together with our old friend, "Oh Susanna", our melody line note always falls on the 1, 2, 3, 4 beat. The tab for the first phrase would look like this:

"Oh Susanna":

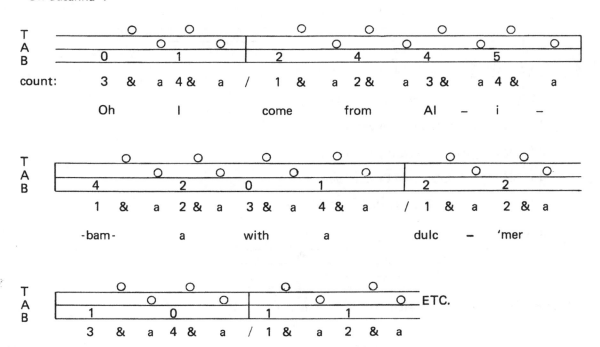

count: 3 & a 4 & a / 1 & a 2 & a 3 & a 4 & a

  Oh   I   come from Al — i —

  1 & a 2 & a 3 & a 4 & a / 1 & a 2 & a

 -bam- a with a dulc — 'mer

  3 & a 4 & a / 1 & a 2 & a

 on my knee _____.

   Here are several other crosspicking patterns. Each one gives the dulcimer a unique sound and can be used to emphasize or accent one string over the others.

<u>2nd Crosspicking Pattern:</u> (melody string emphasis)

  1.) pick the melody string away from you

  2.) pick the bass string towards you

  3.) pick the melody string away from you

  4.) pick the middle string towards you

    (repeat the pattern)

Graphically:

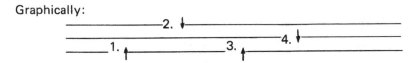

<u>3rd Crosspicking Pattern:</u> (bass string emphasis)

  1.) pick the melody string away from you

  2.) pick the bass string towards you

  3.) pick the middle string away from you

  4.) pick the bass string towards you

    (repeat the pattern)

Graphically:

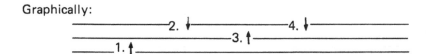

4th Crosspicking Pattern: (middle string emphasis)

1.) pick the melody string away from you

2.) pick the middle string towards you

3.) pick the bass string away from you

4.) pick the middle string towards you

    (repeat the pattern)

Graphically:

5th Crosspicking Pattern: (melody string emphasis)

1.) pick the melody string away from you

2.) pick the middle string towards you

3.) pick the middle string away from you

4.) pick the bass string towards you

    (repeat the pattern)

Graphically:

Very often I'll stutter my patterns with a melody- bass exchange to break the pattern up a little and keep it more interesting. For instance I'll play pattern one through twice then alternate melody- bass and start the pattern over.

6th Crosspicking Pattern: (Melody- bass alternate breakup)

1.) pick the melody string away from you

2.) pick the bass towards you

3.) pick the middle string towards you

4.) pick the melody string away from you

5.) pick the bass string towards you

6.) pick middle string towards you

7.) pick the melody string away from you

8.) pick the bass string towards you

    (repeat the pattern)

Graphically (with count written underneath):

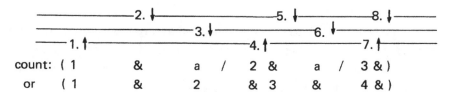

count: (1   &   a   /   2 &   a   /   3 &)
or   (1   &   2   & 3   &   4 &)

As I said earlier, I frequently mix straight strumming and crosspicking, which is what the next two patterns show. The first pattern goes:

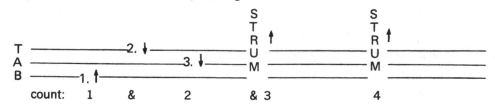

count: 1   &   2   & 3   4

1.   pick away on the melody string

2.   pick towards you on the bass

3.   pick towards on the middle

4.   strum away across all three strings

5.   strum away across all three strings (or strum towards you)

        (Repeat)

A second possible pattern goes:

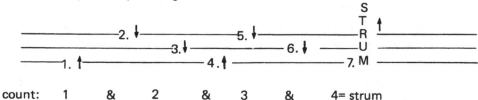

count: 1   &   2   &   3   &   4= strum

1.   pick away on the melody string

2.   pick towards you on the bass

3.   pick towards you on the middle

4.   pick away on the melody string

5.   pick towards you on the bass

6.   pick towards you on the middle

7.   strum away across all three strings

Practice these crosspicking patterns until you feel comfortable with them , then try them out on the songs you already know. For instance, the last pattern above works well with "Sonya's Song".

FINGERPICKING

Please Note: These same exact crosspicking patterns can also be used as finger picking patterns. Pick them as described, but note that instead of the pick hitting each string *the thumb strikes the melody string, while the middle finger plucks the bass string and the index finger picks the middle string.* Generally, though not always, when you finger pick the thumb strikes away from you while the middle and index fingers pick the strings towards you, all three fingers rolling through the pattern in rapid succession. If you feel awkward with the flat-pick, try finger picking and see if it works better for you. If you prefer finger picking and want a little more volume, you can buy plastic thumb-picks and metal finger picks (usually for the banjo) which slip over the tips of your fingers and will sound the strings as loudly as a flat-pick. You can buy finger picks in any good acoustic music store for a few pennies. Another possibility is to buy only the plastic thumb-pick and use it with your "natural" index and middle fingers—if you keep the melody line on the first string this style effectively accents the melody and mutes the drone or chord notes being played behind it on the middle and bass strings. If you want to hear some nice finger-picking, listen to Randy Wilkerson's ELIZABETHAN DULCIMER, also available on the Kicking Mule label (KM-226).

LESSON #4: How To Derive A Melody Line From A Song's Chord Structure

As you venture into the wonderful world of playing with other people, you will sometimes encounter songs that you'll want to learn how to play. Occasionally however, you'll only be presented with the chord structure of the song, particularly if you are learning the piece from a guitar player. Suddenly you'll be faced with the task of constructing your own melody line. In a sense this is completely opposite from everything we've been studying so far; up to now we've worked with the melody and looked at techniques through which to embellish it. In this lesson let's look for a moment at how to "make-up" or fill in a missing melody line.

Before we jump into this technique, let me caution you that it will not work equally well with all songs. Still it will almost always give you some idea of where to go when you are stumped by a missing melody.

The first step will be to learn the chord structure of the song in question. Let's pick an arbitrary chord progression to illustrate the point. The chord pattern goes (in 4/4 time):

D F#m Bm D G C D

We'll assume each chord receives a count of four (one measure = 1, 2, 3, 4), or you can double up on them when first learning the tune and hold each chord for two full measures. Also, let's play each D chord with the same fingering. Normally you would try different fingerings for each chord to see which you prefer sound-wise, but for now let's play them like this: (remember each chord receives the same count)

1. D chord:

2. F#m:

3. Bm: or

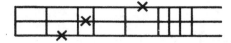 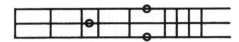

4. D: 5. G:

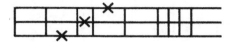 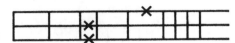

6. C: or

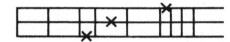 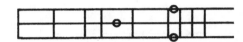

7. D:

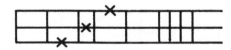

Practice this chord pattern until it feels natural. When you can play through it comfortably, then apply your knowledge of chord inversions and positions to this basic formula. Recall the various forms of D and F♯m for instance:

D chord:

F♯m chord:

With the various chord forms and their inversions in mind, play around with the basic chord pattern and see if you can't find a combination of inversions, which please your ear. Here's how I play the basic chord structure:

(To syncopate the piece a bit, I sometimes leave the first beat of the measure silent, striking the chord form on the second beat, then invert it on the third count and slide up into a higher chord form on the 4th count. At other points I'll simply invert the chord on different beats.)

1. D Chord (first measure) 1st beat silent:

2nd beat   3rd beat

4th beat

2. F#m chord (second measure) played same as above:

2nd beat   3rd beat

4th beat

3. Bm chord (3rd measure) :

1st, 2nd & 3rd beats   4th beat

4. D chord (fourth measure):

first 3 beats   4th beat

5. G chord (fifth measure):

first 3 beats   4th beat

6. C chord (sixth measure):

first 3 beats   4th beat

7. D chord (seventh measure):

1st and 4th beat   2nd and 3rd beat

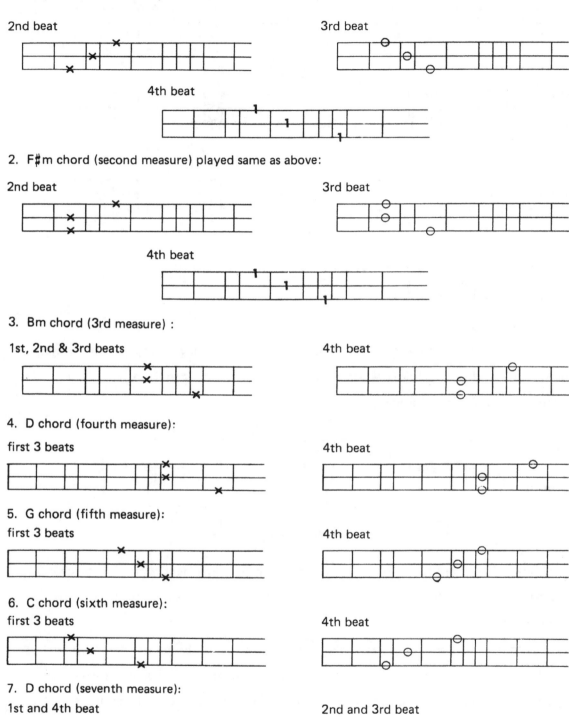

Suddenly, where no melody line existed at all, we find that an implied melody line has emerged from the chord structure itself. To hear the melody by itself, play only the first string in the same order as above. The melody goes:

Implied Melody Line (X= not played)

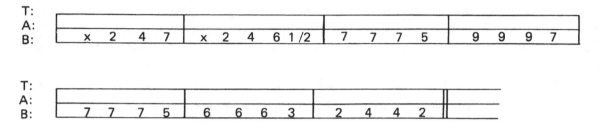

As I said before, this method of implying a missing melody line will not always work, but at the very worst by going through the process you should be able to see alternative ways to play the original chord pattern.

RHYTHM EXERCISE #4:
Use of Tempo & Syncopation In Arranging

In the last section we saw how you can potentially generate a melody line when one is missing. However, there will certainly be times when all you'll really want to do is play the chord structure of a song. Therefore let's look at several different ways to use rhythm chords and syncopation patterns to help arrange a song.

Throughout this book we have stressed rhythm exercises for the simple reason that rhythm is half the whole ballgame; without rhythm there is no music. The mood or feeling of a song frequently comes to us more directly through its tempo and syncopation than through its melody. It's difficult to convey sadness if the tempo of a song is fast and furious, just as it's hard to feel gay when listening to a dirge-like beat. You must consider the feeling contained within a song (whether it was intended to be a country dance or a waltz or a hymn) when you play it. Therefore the **tempo**, the speed at which you play a piece becomes a paramount consideration when you arrange a song. You should always play a new song at several different tempos before settling on one; play it a bit slower and a bit faster than you normally do to see if either variation conveys more completely the feeling which you wish to express. **If you have difficulty keeping time (keeping a steady beat going), you might consider buying yourself a metronome.** A metronome is a mechanical device which beats out a pre-selected tempo for you; you select the speed and then play the song following the metronome's steady beat. Personally, I have found that the rigour and forced routine of working with a metronome has greatly improved my sense of rhythm and timing. The ability to set this device at varying speeds can help you decide at what tempo you want to play a song.

Initially playing a new song with a straight forward rhythmic pattern is probably a good idea. However, when you are a bit more familiar with a tune and feel you have a better handle on what it has to say as well as what you want to express through the song (and ultimately this is what music is all about: pleasurable self-expression), then you can begin to play around with the song's rhythmic structure by syncopating it.

Syncopation means you displace or accent certain chosen beats within the rhythmic structure; i.e., you drop or add beats and accent more forcefully or weakly certain beats within a measure. In short, you give the rhythmic structure of a song (4/4, 3/4 time, etc.) a different inflection pattern from the normal straight forward one beat = one strum approach. Accordingly, let's run through an exercise designed to show you how to take a 4/4 rhythm and break it up into various syncopated rhythms simply by varying the strumming pattern. In the diagram below I present only one measure's worth of a selected rhythmic variation, but you should play each one until you feel comfortable with the new strumming pattern. For the purpose of this exercise, strike the chord once for every (/) slanted line. Two //'s together are counted as 1 &, so strum away from you on 1 and towards yourself on &. Three ///'s are counted as a **triplet**: 1 & a; so strum away, towards, then away again (rapidly since you must fit the triplet into the same time span you normally give to 1 beat.) Go slowly and follow the patterns carefully, changing chords when indicated. We are still in the Mixolydian key of D.

Basic Straight Forward Strumming Patterns:

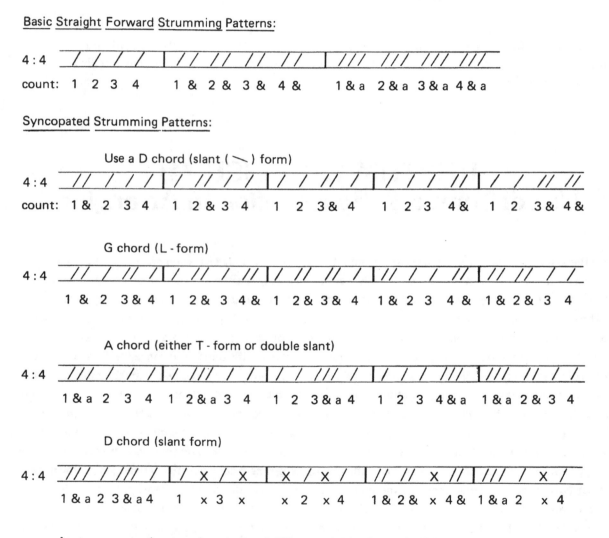

As you can see there are hundreds of different rhythmic possibilities-- make up your own to fit your songs. Obviously, you can also string a group of these patterns together to fit a phrase or a part of a song. Once again the method of divide and reform to conquer works well. Let's look at "Oh Susanna" one last time to see how we can fit several syncopated rhythmic patterns behind it to give its phrases different feelings. Follow the strumming lines (/) beneath the melody and above the tab.

"Oh Susanna"
(Syncopated)

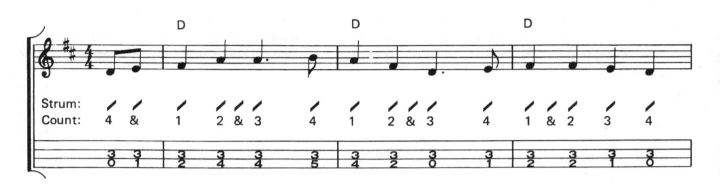

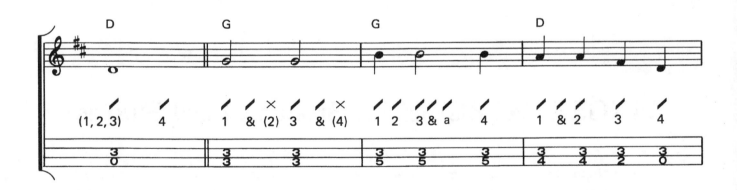

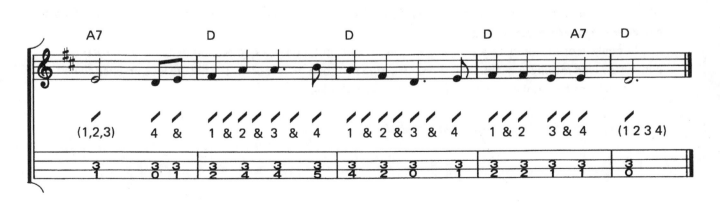

When working with rhythmic patterns to arrange a song, you have two clear choices: 1.) You can choose a syncopation pattern (or a mixed but fixed pattern) and then stick with it throughout the chord changes in the song; or 2.) You can vary the rhythmic strumming patterns to fit the feel of the melody line behind which you're strumming the chord structure. With the first choice you are playing **rhythm dulcimer**, while in tthe second instance you are simply backing up the melody with the chords. If you are singing or playing rhythm behind a lead line player, you'll probably want to stay with the first choice, and try to keep a steady rhythmic pattern going.

FINGER EXERCISE #4: Broken Chord Studies

We have been studying the means to infer melody lines from chord structures, as well as ways to use only the chord structure of a song to arrange it. One way to unite both of these possibilities is to look at a technique which breaks a chord down into its separate notes. **When you strike the separate notes which make up a chord one after the other you are playing an arpeggio.**

Not only does this produce a pleasant harp like sound, but it offers another possibility for constructing improvised lead melody lines from the chord structure of a song. To limber up our fingers let's practice some chord arpeggios by running through a few **broken chord studies**.

Broken Chord Studies: (key of D, Mixolydian Mode)

Broken Chord Studies

Some of these exercises are written 8va (one octave higher) then they are actually played, for ease of sight reading.

TRANSPOSITION:
How to Move a Song from One Key to Another.

As you learn how to read music, and I highly encourage you to do so since it will open up a great wealth of music which you might otherwise never have access to (see the appendix on "Reading Music"), you will time and again run into songs written in keys which call for you to retune your dulcimer. Assuming you don't want to be constantly retuning your instrument, you will need to know a little about transposing: the method of quickly and easily translating one key into another. In time you will be able to look at a song and transpose it on sight into one of the keys encompassed by the Mixolydian Mode, Key of D tuning.

First however, you must learn to tell what key a song is written in. The sharps (#'s) and flats (b's) found on the bar stave directly to the right of the treble clef (🎼) tell you what key a song is written in. Here are the twelve possible keys:

=C (no #'s or b's)

=G (one # = F#)

=D (F#, C#)

=A (F#, C#, G#)

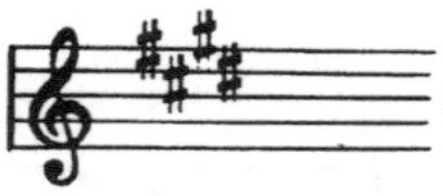

=E (F#, C#, G#, D#)

=B (F#, C#, G#, D#, A#)

=F#(F#, C#, G#, D#, A#, E#)

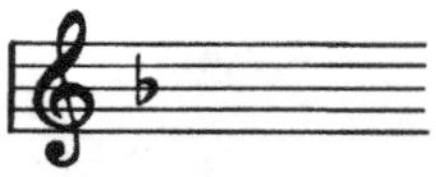

=F (one b= Bb)

=Bb(Bb, Eb)

=Eb(Bb, Eb, Ab)

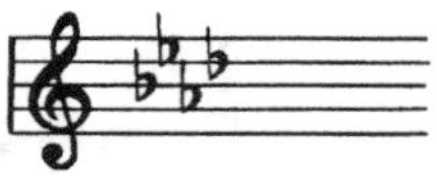

=Ab(Bb, Eb, Ab, Db)

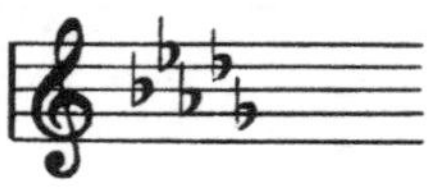

=Db(Bb, Eb, Ab, Db, Gb)

Once you are able to identify the song's key you can decide which key you want to transpose it into. For instance, if you are confronted by a song with two b's (key of Bb) you might choose to drop each note one half step and so transpose the song into the key of A (readily playable in the D tuning). In this case you simply start the song by playing the first note one-half step lower than it is written on the page. If the opening note of the song is Bb, you would play the A note (at the 4th fret); if it is Eb you would play a D note either at the 7th fret or in the open position on the first string. Hereafter the interval between melody notes remains the same as that found in the original. **Note:** Remember there is 1/2 step between each of the 12 notes in a chromatic octave.

You could just as easily choose to transpose the Bb song into the key of D raising each note of the melody line a step and a half. In this instance the opening Bb note would become a D note (open string or 7th fret); and the Eb note would become an F# note (played at the 2nd or the 9th frets). **In effect, once you decide how many steps or half-steps up or down you wish to move (transpose) the opening melody line note, each successive note thereafter moves this same distance, thereby maintaining the original whole and half-step intervals between each melody line notes.**

Here are a couple of examples:

Photo by **Mark Biggs**

"Oh Susanna"
(Transpositions)

Mixolydian Mode
1st phrase

Key B♭

To play this as is
we would have to
tune
(B♭ B♭ E♭ b♭ B♭)

So we Transpose it into:

Key A

(1/2 step
drop) tuned
(D D A D)

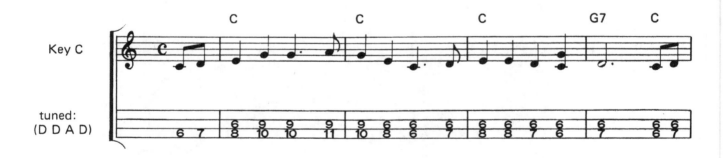

Key C

tuned:
(D D A D)

Transposed into:

Key D

(1 step raised
tuned:
(D D A D)

* Note: We could also play this as we learned the song, starting on the open melody string instead of one
octave higher (8va) at the 7th as shown here.

Typically, when I am transposing into the Mixolydian Mode key of D, I'll follow these patterns:

Key of F into Key of G: raise each note 1 full step

Key of Bb into Key of A: lower each note 1/2 step

Key of Eb into Key of D: lower each note 1/2 step

Key of E into Key of D: lower each note 1 step

    or into Key of A: raise each note 2 & 1/2 steps

Key of C into Key of D: raise each note 1 step

You may feel intimidated at first by transposing, but in short order you should be able to see that the dulcimer by way of its fixed tunings and diatonic (7 tone) fretboard is uniquely well suited to moving from one key into another with little difficulty. Your original choice as to which key to move into (how many steps or half steps you'll move each note) will determine how easy or difficult the transposition will turn out to be. So if transposing seems unduly difficult, consider trying another key before giving up entirely. Be aware also that if a song is unplayable in the original key due to its chromatic content, it will remain unplayable no matter how you try to transpose it.

REVIEW OF ARRANGING TECHNIQUES:

Before we move into another tuning and leave the Mixolydian Mode behind, let's very briefly review the many different string techniques we've discussed as possible ways to arrange a song. Clearly the two basic building blocks of any song are its melody line and rhythmic structure. Therefore we can begin to shape or arrange any new song by dealing directly with these two fundamental elements. Once we know the melody line we can put the full or partial chord structure of the piece behind it; we can play the melody backed by split octave and set chords or by harmony 3rds, and 5ths ; we can flat-pick the melody line across all three strings; or we can use a cross-picking pattern to meld the melody together with the song's chord structure. Knowing the chord structure of the tune we can play back-up rhythm dulcimer by following a steady rhythmic pattern, or we can introduce syncopation and varied rhythms to change the mood of the song; we can transpose the song into a different time signature (3/4 into 6/8, or 4/4 into 3/4, etc.) or into a different key; or we can create an "alternative" melody line by playing a series of broken chord patterns. We also have a wide variety of string effects which we can bring into use to accent certain notes or passages, or to set certain moods. These techniques include: tremelo, slides, bends, hammer-ons and pull-offs, harmonics, finger brushing, and bowing.

The general idea is to use not only one but many of these techniques in every song, experimenting constantly to discover what combination best enables us to express our thoughts and feelings through a song's unique arrangement. All of these techniques also work equally well in each of the different Modes or tunings which we are about to explore, so please continue to use them freely in the following sections.

Photo by Mark Biggs

108

TWENTY-TWO SONGS FOR THE MIXOLYDIAN MODE

(Intermediate to Advanced)

This is a great old capstan sea chantey, used when the order was given to set sail on the sailing ships. The sailors would gather about the capstan, the big winch used to raise the anchor from the deep six, where they'd sing songs to keep their timing all together, or maybe just to keep their spirits flying high in the good salt sea breeze. It flows along smoothly at a moderate pace.

"Maid of Amsterdam" (A-Roving)

1st Printed 1608
English
Sea Chantey

Maid of Amsterdam (A-Roving)

In Amsterdam there dwells a maid,
  Mark well what I do say;
In Amsterdam there dwells a maid,
  And she is mistress of her trade.

Chorus:
    I'll go no more a-roving
    With you, fair maid.
    A-roving, a-roving,
    Since roving's been my ru-in,
    I'll go no more a-roving
    With you, fair maid.

Her eyes are blue, her cheeks are red,
  Mark well what I do say;
Her eyes are blue, her cheeks are red,
  A wealth of hair is on her head.

I put my arm around her waist,
  Mark well what I do say;
I put my arm around her waist,
  Says she, "Young man, you're in some haste."

I took that girl upon my knee,
  Mark well what I do say;
I took that girl upon my knee,
  Says she, "Young man, you're rather free."

She swore that she'd be true to me,
  Mark well what I do say;
She swore that she'd be true to me,
  Then spent my money both fast and free.

    I'll go no more a-roving
    with you, fair maid.

"The Irish Washerwoman"

112

This lovely Welsh air flows along sweetly and smoothly, graceful as the gently rolling green hills of Wales. The lady must have been truely delightful.

"Lady Owen's Delight"

Mix. D
(key of G)

18th Cent. Welsh Air

"The Lass of Gowrie"

I must thank Robin Williamson of the Incredible String Band fame for introducing me on to many fine old folksongs, not the least of them being these three"Lass" tunes. I have a particular fondness for old country dance tunes which seem to capture the best spirits of those long lost days. This lass must have been dark eyed and charming, much quieter than her counterpart, the ''Lass of Patie's Mill'', a song I often play together with this one. Written by James Hook before 1787, this English dance tune goes smoothly and not too fast-for the love of a young lady should never be rushed.

"The Lass of Richmond Hill"

18th Cent. Eng.

Mix. D

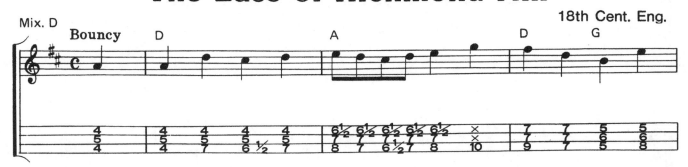

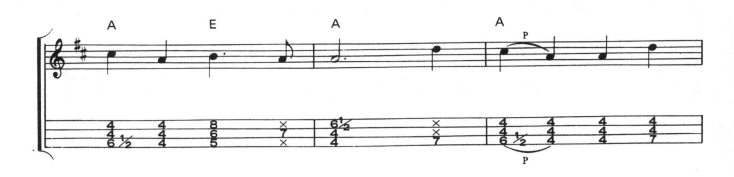

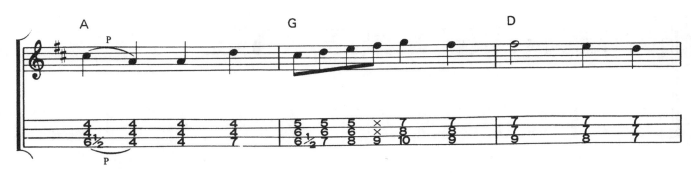

115

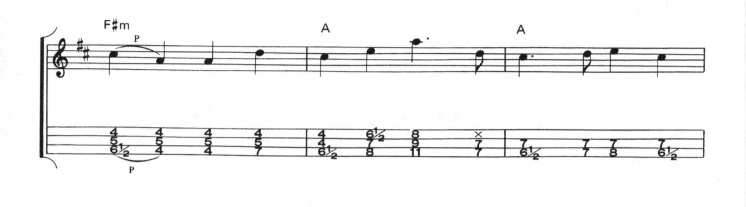

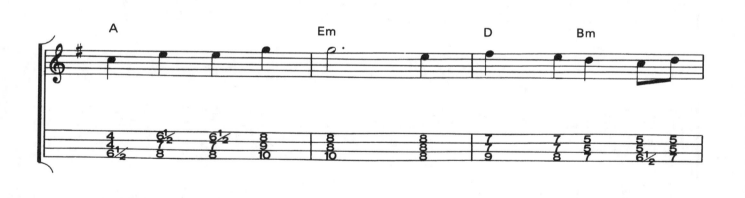

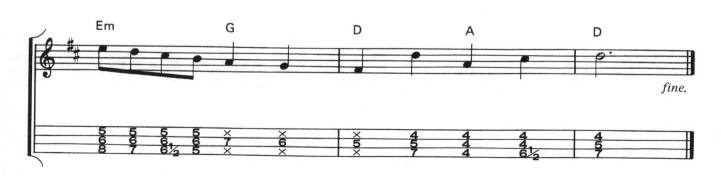

Originally printed in Thompson's ORPHEUS CALEDONIUS in 1725, this lovely Scottish dance tune should reel and bounce along at a good clip. She must have been a spirited lass, full of fun and laughter.

"The Lass of Patie's Mill"

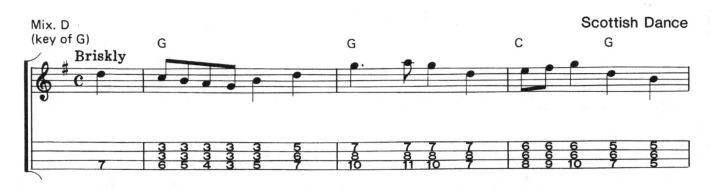

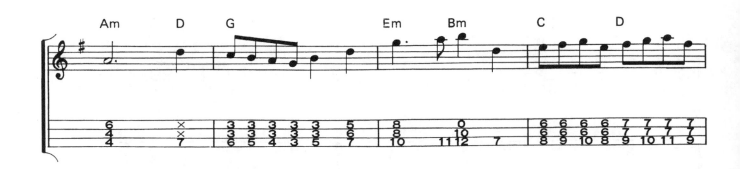

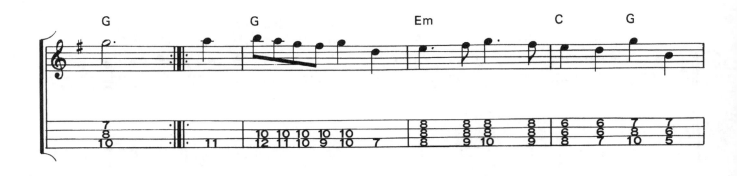

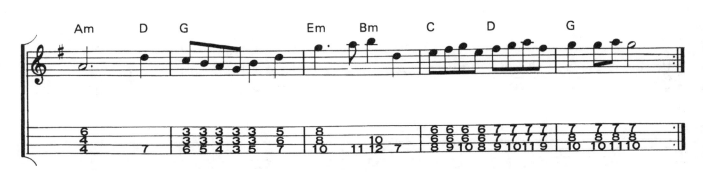

Hey's have been around since the 16th century. They are a variation of the line dances which form a large part of the country dance repetoire. English in origin, the hey goes along moderately fast and well accented as the dancers braid themselves up a long line, interweaving in a sort of human braid. I can almost hear everyone, dancers and musicians alike, giving a rousing shout of "hey" when the music turns 'round upon itself.

"The Shepherd's Hey"

18th Cent. Eng.
Country Dance

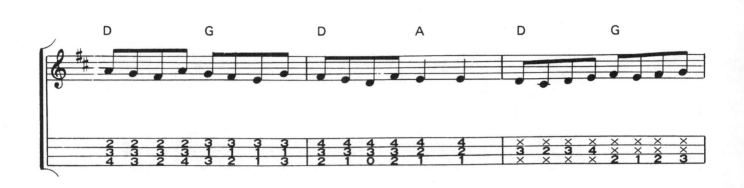

(3rd part)

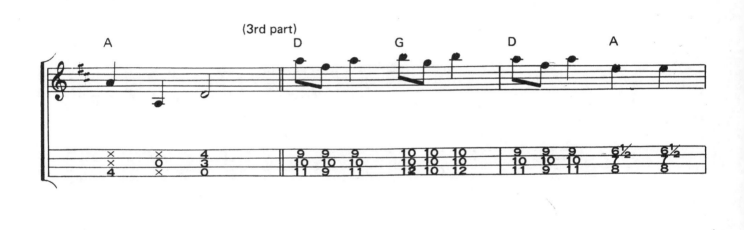

(4th part)

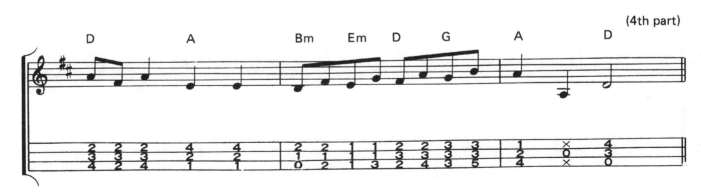

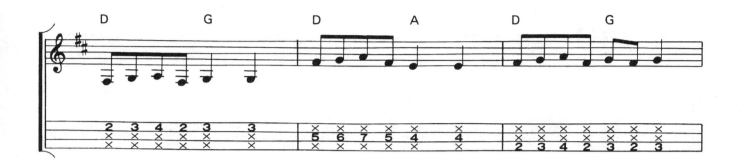

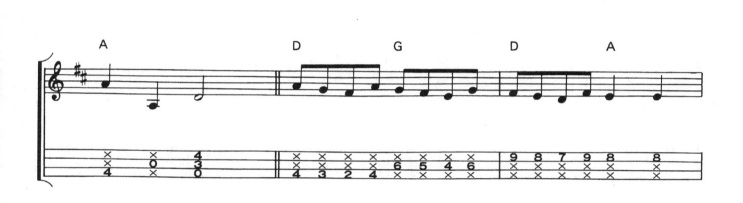

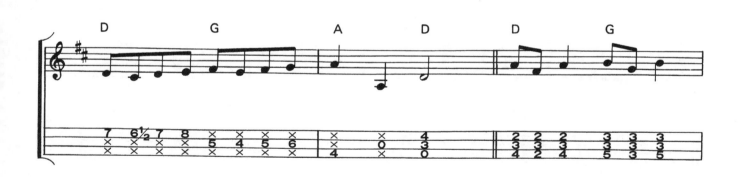

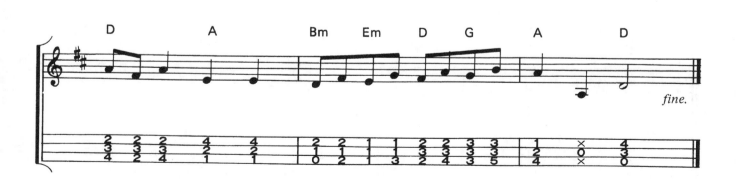

fine.

"The Handsome Couple"

121

122

"Linnen Hall"

This tune moves happily along to greet the new day. Play it with gusto & a proud toss of the head.

"The Dawning of the Day"
(or "The Golden Star")

Mix. D
Key A

Thomas Connelan (circa 1660)

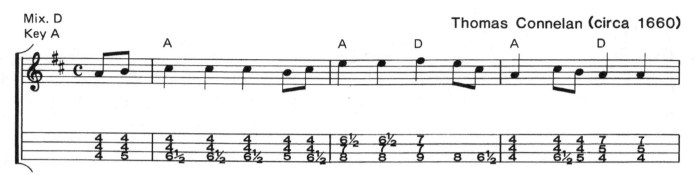

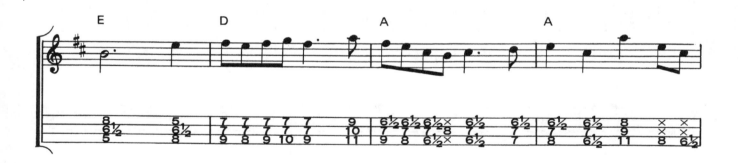

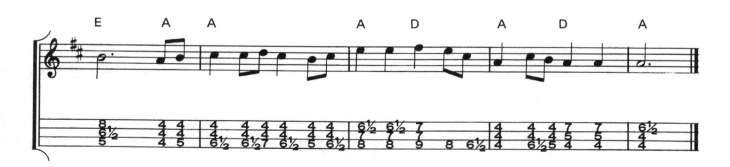

124

"La Paloma"
(Full Chord Version)

Mixolydian D

Classical Spanish, Mid 1800's
Sebastion Yradir

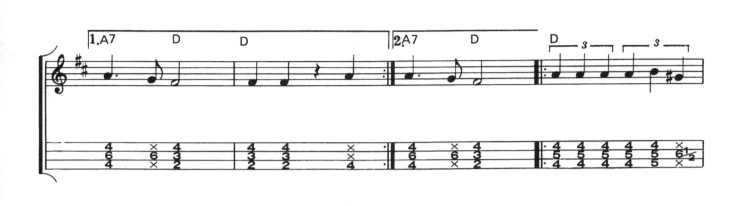

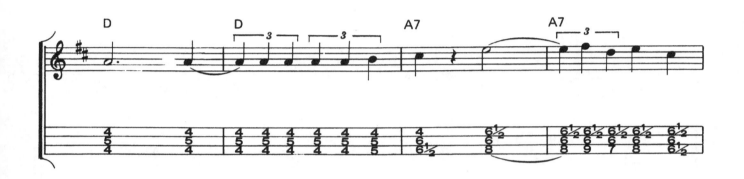

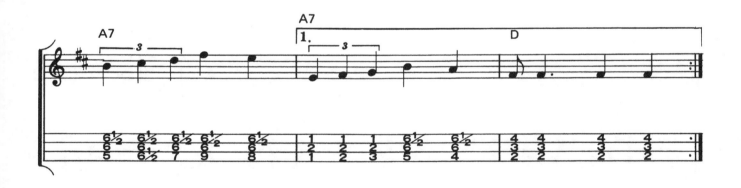

(Harmonic at 14th)

fine.

126

Play this one with feeling, gently during part A and with gusto in part B, mellowing out for the feinal refrain.
I can't tell you why, but the color blue always gloods my mind when I hear a song in the key of Bm hence the title:

"Improvisation on a Blue Mood"

Mix. D
(Key Bm)

by Mark Biggs

127

Mark Biggs

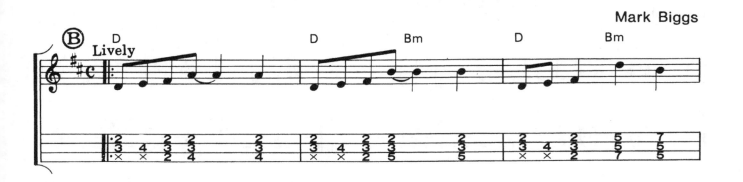

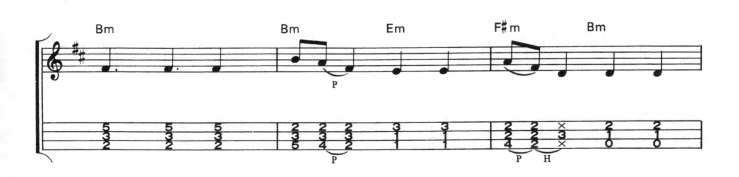

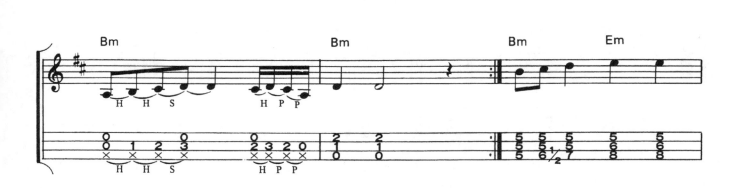

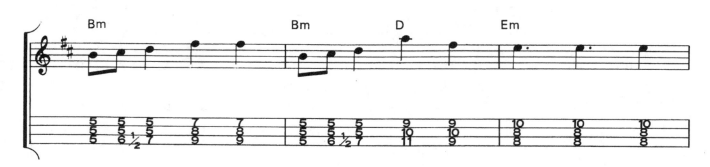

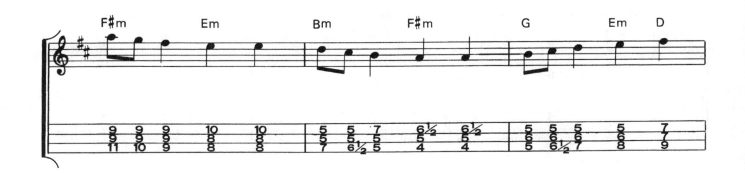

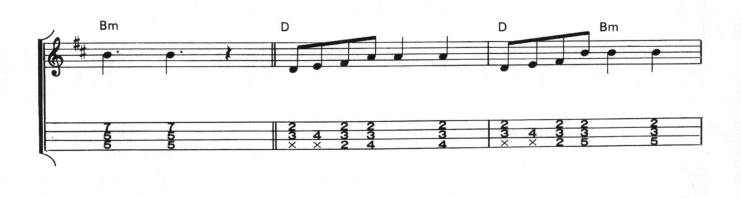

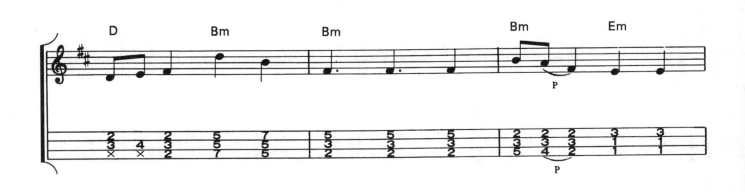

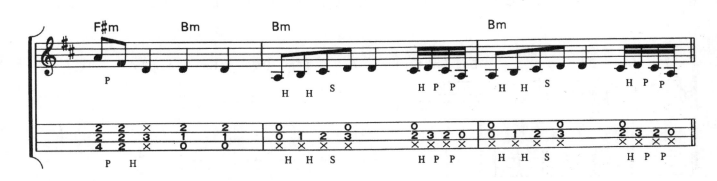

130

This is a remarkably sad but beautiful song. The wistful, almost melancholy mood of the anonymous composer is laid bare upon the page for us all to experience. Play this one with all the heart you can put into it.

Mix. D
(key Bm)

"Fuge In Bm"

Smoothly

17th Cent. Lute Song

132

Another lute tune from the Golden Age of lute music, "What If A Day" was printed as early as 1603. It is a lovely tune with a feeling of Spring in it, perhaps even a hint of love - sickness lingering about in its minor chords; a sensation which spring has sometimes been known to summon forth in many a winter weary heart.

"What If A Day"

Mix. D
(key Am)

16th Cent. Eng. Lute Song

133

John Dowland (1563 - 1626) was a virtuoso without equal on the lute in an period known as the "Golden Age of the Lute" (1580 - 1620). This Englishman was a remarkable composer as well, judging from this lively, happy tune which comes from one of his many Lute books.

"Wilson's Wilde"

John Dowland
Elizabethan Lute Song
16th Cent.

Two Renaissance Lute Pieces

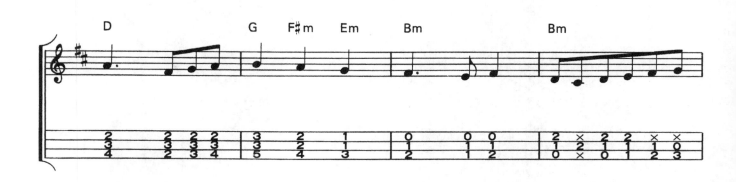

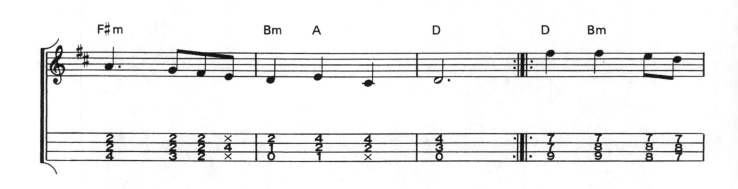

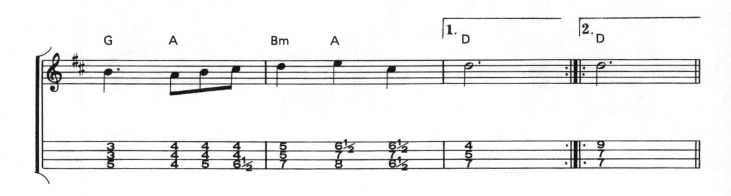

Photo by Mark Biggs

I wrote this tune one evening after watching a show about a little boy named Adam who was kidnapped and murdered in the '70's. Actually the inspiration for the piece came from the parents of this child who managed to survive the ordeal and eventually find the trust, hope, faith and love to have another child. They named her Meagan Jayne. This song goes slowly, and sweetly, with a full measure of love.

"Meagan Jayne"

Mix. D
(key Bm)

Slowly with feeling

Mark Biggs

I frequently make a medley out of Meagan Jayne & Planxty Irwin since their moods work so well together. One of O'Carolan's most popular & accessible songs - give you whole heart over to it.

"Planxty Irwin"

Mix. D

Turlough O'Carolon

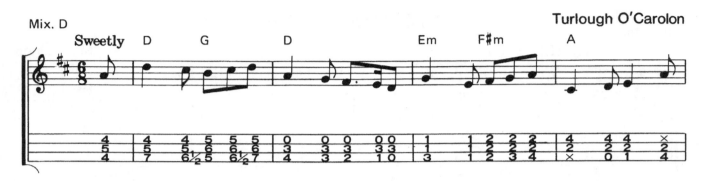

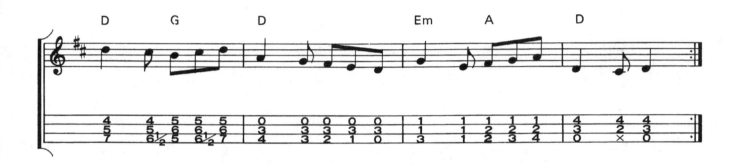

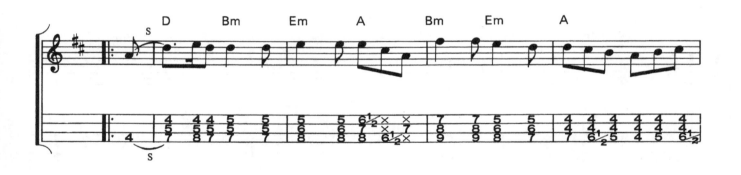

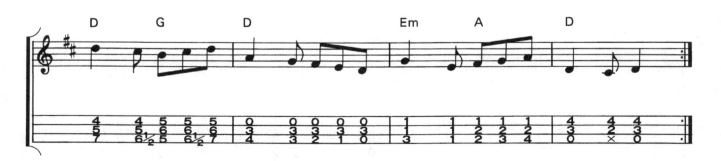

"Planxty Morgan Magan"

Turlough O'Carolan

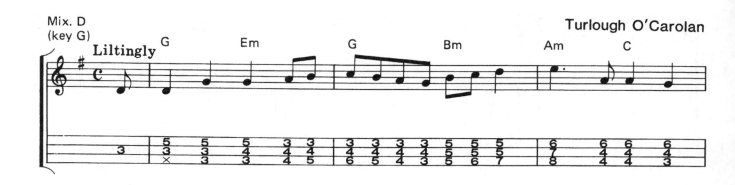

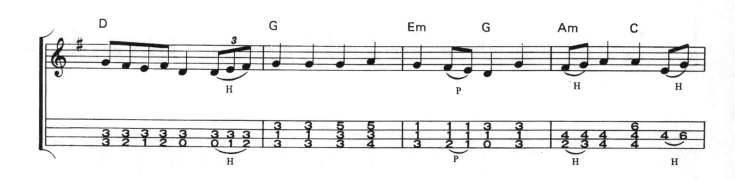

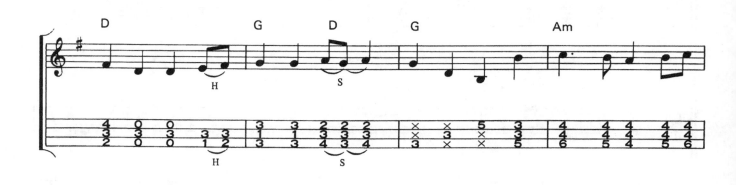

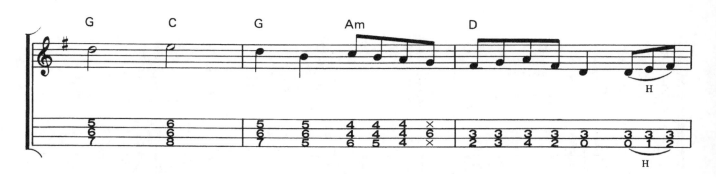

142

Turlough O'Carolan was born in Ireland in 1670. Undoubtedly destined to follow in his father's footsteps and enter the ironworking business, he was left blind by a severe case of smallpox at the age of eighteen. With the help of the wife of his father's boss, Mrs MacDermott Roe, Turlough began to study the Celtic harp and within two years began his lifelong pursuit of music. One of the greatest of the Irish harpers, he composed over two thousand songs before his death some fifty years later in 1738. Roughly spanning the era of Johann Sebastian Bach (1685 - 1750), O'Carolan was as important to the furthering of Irish harp music as Bach was to the formation of Baroque music. He is one of my musical heroes, and his tunes are among my favorite dulcimer songs. They are challenging but always fulfiling, and inevitably seem to release the magic and emotion which must have originally entered into their creation. "Lord Inchiquin", written for the fourth Earl of Inchiquin in County Clare, Ireland, flows along regally at a moderate pace— to my ears it has a baroque quality to it.

"Lord Inchiquin"

Turlough O'Carolan

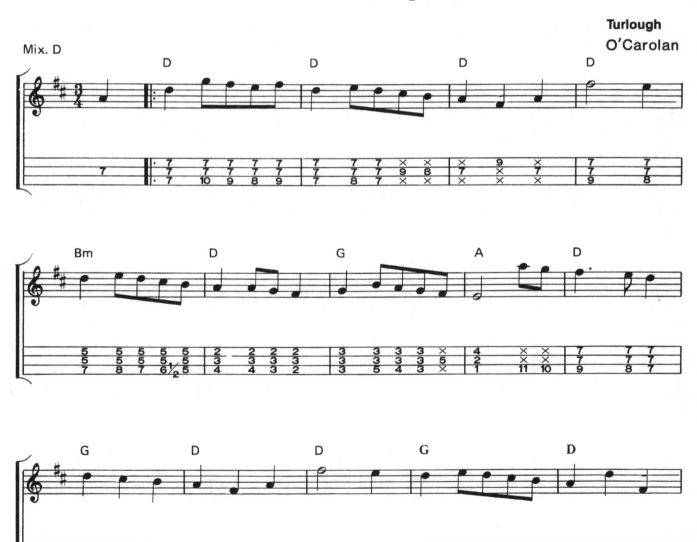

143

144

This most beautiful, and difficult Irish harp tune was written by Rory Dall O'Cathain sometime in the first half of the 17th Century. O'Cathain was an Irish Baron who moved to Scotland as was the vogue in those days, and later became friends with King James the VI of England. He wrote this lovely air, "Da Mihi Manum" in reply to an apology offered him by the Lady Eglinton who had unintentionally insulted him one day. It seems he had arrived from a days walk through the heather at her castle unannounced. When she learned he was a harper of some reknown, she had demanded a tune from him, a grave breech of etiquette. He left the castle in a royal huff and only afterwards did she discover her error, whereupon she wrote him a letter of heartfelt apology. Or at least I assume this to have been the case, judging from his very gentle and loving response. Play this air lightly with much feeling.

"Give Me Your Hand"

Rory Dall O'Cathain
17th Cent. Harp
Irish Air

Note: 6/4 is played like 6/8 but counted: 1 2 3, 4 5 6.

* This is where the piece ends 2nd or 3rd time through.

145

146

Here's my concession to good old rock and roll, one of my undeniable musical influences. It goes just about as fast as humanly (or humanely) possible. It's happy to be moving on, wandering down the road as I was for several years. If you have a metronome set it at 184 & follow me if you dare or care to.

"Maybe You'll Wander"

Mark Biggs

147

148

149

150

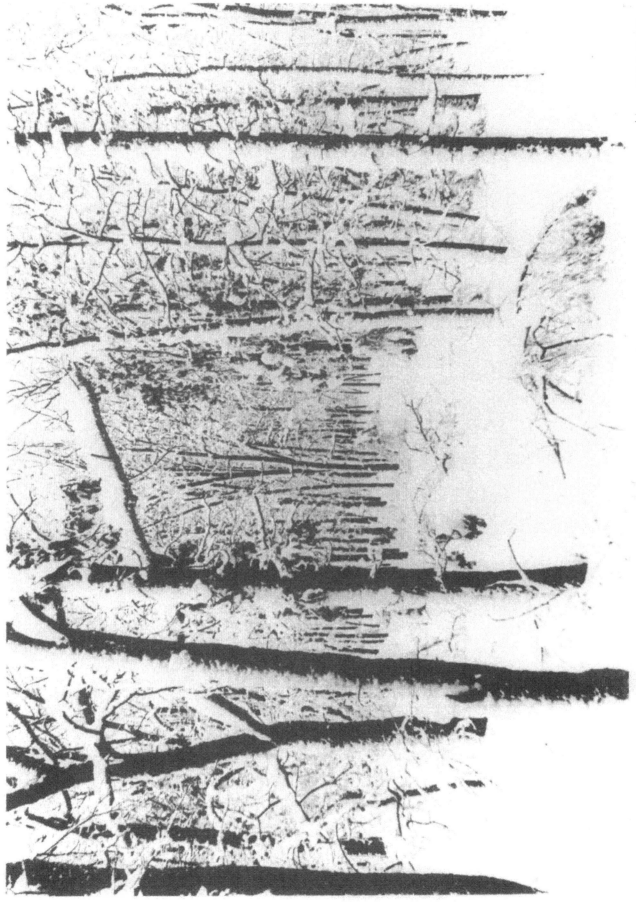

151

PART TWO:

THE IONIAN MODE VS. THE NEW IONIAN MODE

The Ionian Mode is a major mode comprised of a completely major scale (no flattened sixth like we encounter in the Mixolydian Mode). It is perhaps the most traditional dulcimer tuning and a great many dulcimer standards have been written for this mode. Unfortunately, because the melody and the middle strings share the exact same note in this tuning, the Ionian doesn't allow us the freedom to either invert our chords or to walk a melody line across the fretboard. Overall I find the Ionian far less flexible than the Mixolydian Mode, and it is for this reason that I normally tune into the New Ionian Mode when I wish to take advantage of the Ionian's peculiar voice and unique chording possibilities.

The New Ionian Mode differs from the Standard Ionian in this way: the note which the bass string is normally tuned to moves to the middle string in the New Ionian, while the middle string's note shifts across to the bass string position and drops one octave in tone. The diagram below should make this clear. The real advantage to the New Ionian tuning is that by retaining the octave split between the bass and the melody string we can continue to invert our chords and to walk melodies across all three strings of the dulcimer. Maintaining the octave split also means that it is very easy to retune from the Mixolydian into the New Ionian Mode: all you do is drop the middle string one full step, fretting it at the fourth (instead of at the third) to get the same tone as the first string played open.

TUNING INTO THE IONIAN AND NEW IONIAN MODE:

As always, you must first select your keytone, the key you wish to tune into. Since we are already tuned in the Mixolydian key of D, let's make it easy and tune into the New Ionian key of G.

In the **Standard Ionian Mode** the bass string is tuned to the keytone first; the note on the bass string always tells you what key you are tuned in. Once you have brought the bass string to the desired note, fret it at the fourth fret and tune both the middle and melody strings that tone.

In the **New Ionian Mode** the middle string is tuned to the keytone (and consequently tells you what key you are tuned in). So first tune the middle string to the desired note, then fret it at the fourth fret and bring the melody string to this exact same tone. Once you've done this, fret the bass string at the seventh and tune it to the same tone as the first string played open. You can double check the bass by fretting it at the third and making sure it has the same tone as the middle string played open. **(Note: To tune into the New Ionian from the Mixolydian, simply fret the middle string at the fourth fret (instead of at the 3rd) and tune it to the Melody string played open. The melody & bass strings remain unchanged.)**

STANDARD IONIAN MODE:

Melody	Middle	Bass	Key
CC	C	F	(F)
DD	D	G	(G)
EE	E	A	(A)
(1)	(1)	(4)	

153

NEW IONIAN MODE:

	CC	F	C	(F)
We'll tune here:	**DD**	**G**	**D**	**(G)**
	EE	A	E	(A)
	(1)	(4)	(8)	

Many of the chord patterns used in the Mixolydian Mode will be encountered in the New Ionian tuning. It is important to remember that while these patterns share the same fingering, they form different chords. You must remember that the middle string is tuned one full step lower than in the Mixolydian; i.e. the middle string position for every chord you learned in the Mix. will now be fingered one full step (one large fret) higher up the fretboard. Take a look at the New Ionian chords in the back of this book. I think you will find it quite easy to re-orient yourself to this mode because of its many similarities to the Mixolydian Mode. Here are a couple of songs in the Ionian Mode and several in the New Ionian to let you see how they differ in fingering from the Mixolydian Mode.

"Hand Me Down My Walking Cane"

Ionian G
(DD D G)

Trad. Am Folksong

* Note: You can easily Translate any standard Ionian song into the New Ionian mode by simply switching the fingering posititions of the middle string with the bass string.

155

Hand Me Down My Walking Cane

Oh, hand me down my walking cane,
Yes, hand me down my walking cane.
Well hand me down my walking cane
I'm going to leave on the midnight train,
All my friends been taken away, taken away.

Oh hand me down my liquor jug,
Yes, hand me down my liquor jug.
Well hand me down my liquor jug
I'm gonna drink till I'm sober as a judge,
All my friends been taken away, taken away.

Oh I got drunk and I landed in jail,
Yes, I got drunk and landed in jail.
Well I got drunk and landed in jail,
Got nobody for to go my bail,
All my friends been taken away, taken away.

So hand me down my walking shoes,
Yes, hand me down my walking shoes.
Now hand me down my walking shoes,
I'm gonna walk away these blues,
All my friends been taken away, taken away.

"Shenandoah"

Shenandoah

Oh Shenandoah, I love your daughter.
   A-way, my rolling river!
I'll take her 'cross your rolling waters.
   A-way, we're bound a-way,
   'Cross the wide Missouri.

Oh, Shenandoah, I long to hear you,
   A-way, my rolling river!
'Cross that wide and rolling river.
   A-way, we're bound away,
   'Cross the wide Missouri.

Oh, Shenandoah, I'll ne'er forget you,
   A-way, my rolling river!
Till the day I die, I'll love you ever.
   A-way, we're bound away,
   'Cross the wide Missouri.

"Go To Jane Glover"

"Cripple Creek"

New Ionian G

Trad. Am.

Cripple Creek

Chorus:

    Going up to Cripple Creek, going on the run,
    Going up to Cripple Creek to have a little fun.
    Going up to Cripple Creek, going in a whirl,
    Going up to Cripple Creek to see my little girl.

I got a gal at the head of the creek,
Going up to see her 'bought the middle of the week.
Kiss her on the mouth just as sweet as any wine,
Wrap herself around me like a sweet potater vine.

Cripple Creek's cold and Cripple Creek's deep,
I'll wade old Cripple Creek 'fore I sleep.
The road is rocky and the hillside's steep,
I'll have blisters all over my feet.

Photo by Mark Biggs

"Hark The Herald Angels Sing"

New Ionian G
(D D G D)

Felix Mendelssohn

"O' Keefe's Slide"

* Slides are broken into four groups of triplets, counted: 1 2 3, 1 2 3, 1 2 3, 1 2 3, They "reel" along like a tipsy man at pub's closing.

163

"Planxty Fanny Power"

18th Cent. Irish
Turlough O'Carolan

"Farewell"

New Ionian G

Liltingly

Trad. Scottish Air

* This lonely air makes a good companion piece with "Fanny Powers".

"Arabesque" grew out of the opening few bars of the melody line one gray winter day last year when sunshine and thoughts of escaping south across the border lay heavy on my mind. Max Tyndall, my good friend and sometime musical ally, helped me broaden the theme over the course of several months, until this final version peaked its head up with the first few spring daffodils. By that time the urge to flee to warmer climes had left me and I found myself bent over to smell the first flowers of spring, in a posture something akin to a ballet dancers pose--the "arabesque". Then again the piece is also a 'fantasy', an intricate interweaving of a basic melodic figure-- once again an "arabesque". It definitely has a Mexican mood about it; play it liltingly at a moderate speed.

"Arabesque"

Mexican Feel
New Ionian G

Mark Biggs & Max Tyndall

* I play this note as a rapid triplet 4 5 4 by hammering on & pulling off very
rapidly before sliding down to the 3rd fret.

166

167

168

169

THE AEOLIAN MODE: A Minor Tuning

So far we have worked only with major sounding modes. Let's look now at the minor tuning known as the Aeolian (A-O-lian) Mode. This mode utilizes the normal minor scale with its flattened third (see the appendix on Major and Minor Scales). It is a lovely tuning that seems particularly well suited to medieval and Renaissance folk tunes, though almost any song written in a minor key sounds great in the Aeolian.

Tuning:

Once again as in the Ionian Mode, we tune our bass string to the desired keytone (and again the name of the minor key we are in comes from the note found on the bass string). When you have the bass string tuned to the proper pitch, fret it at the fourth and tune the middle string to this tone. Now fret the bass string at the 6th fret and tune the open melody string to this tone. **To tune into the Aeolian from the Mixolydian** it is simpler to simultaneously fret the melody string at the first fret and the middle string at the third fret. Now bring these two string to the exact same tone, either lowering the melody string one full step to the tone of the middle string, or raising the middle string one full step up to the pitch of the melody string. Finally tune the bass string to the same tone as the melody fretted at the first or the middle fretted at the third fret. **Note:** If you lowered the melody string one step, the bass string will not have to be retuned; if you raised the middle string one step, you will also raise the bass string one full step. For a final double check, all three strings should have the same tone when the first string is fretted at the first and the middle string is simultaneously fretted at the third.

AEOLIAN MODE:	Melody	Middle	Bass	Key
	DD	B	E	(Em)
	CC	A	D	(Dm)
	BbBb	G	C	(Cm)
	(1)	(6)	(9)	

Here are a few hauntingly beautiful songs to help get you started playing in the Aeolian Mode.

"The Black Nag"

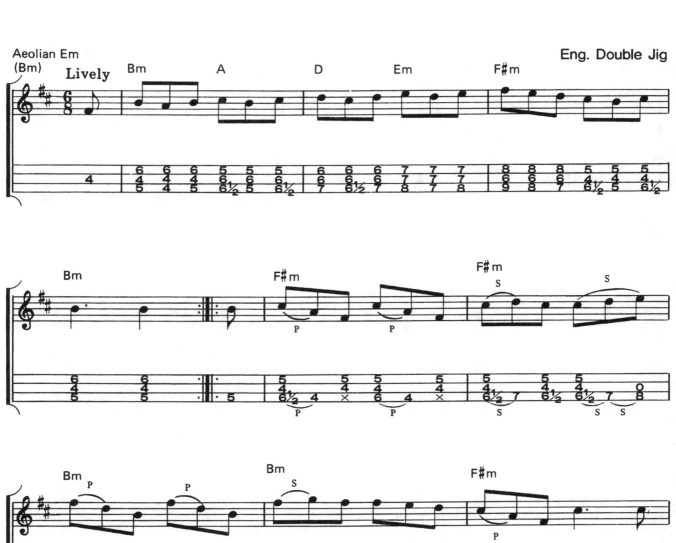

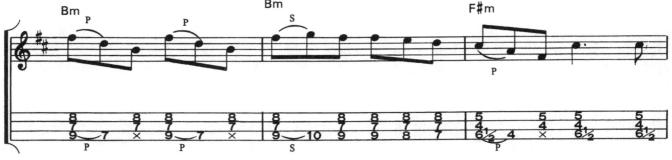

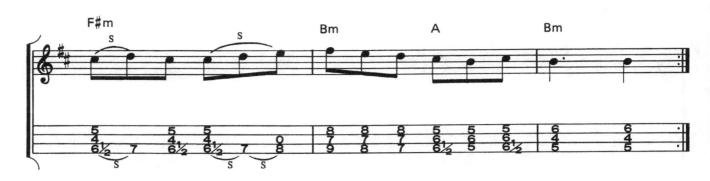

"Shady Grove"

Eng. Folk Song

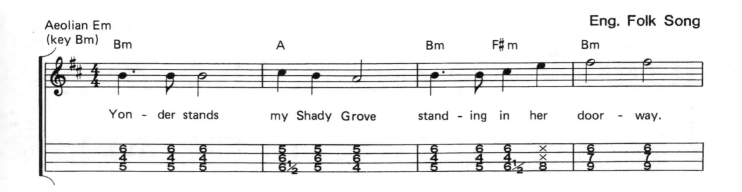

Yon - der stands my Shady Grove stand - ing in her door - way.

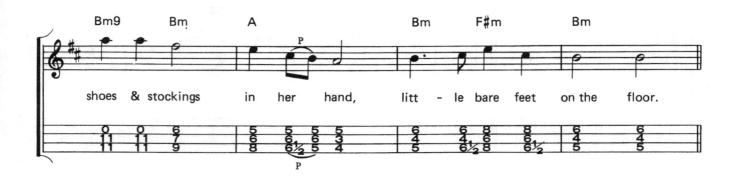

shoes & stockings in her hand, litt - le bare feet on the floor.

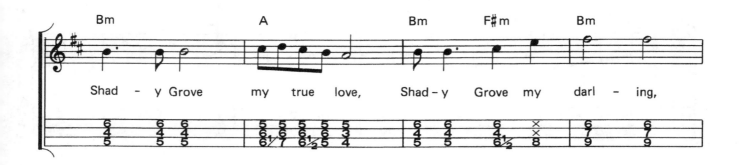

Shad - y Grove my true love, Shad - y Grove my darl - ing,

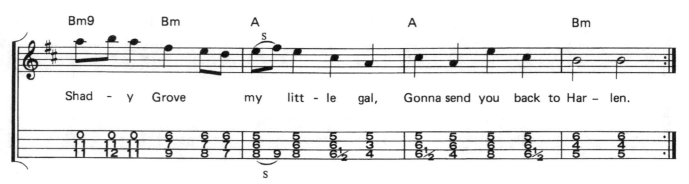

Shad - y Grove my litt - le gal, Gonna send you back to Har - len.

Shady Grove

Chorus:
  Shady Grove my little love,
  Shady Grove my darling,
  Shady Grove my little gal,
  Gonna send you back to Harlen.

Yonder stands my Shady Grove,
Standing in her doorway.
Shoes and stockings in her hand,
Little bare feet on the floor.

Some come here to fiddle and play,
Some come here to marry.
Some come here to fiddle and play,
I come here to marry.

Wish I had me a banjo string,
Made of golden twine.
Every tune I'd pluck on it'd be
Wish that gal was mine.

Peaches in the summertime,
Apples in the fall.
If I can't have the gal I love,
Don't want none at all.

"Scarborough Fair"

English Folk Song

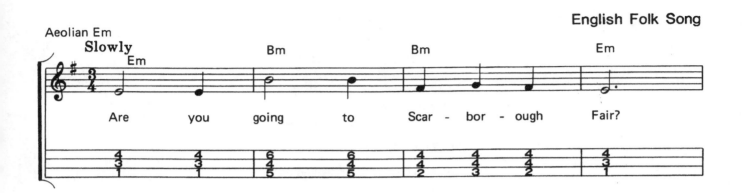

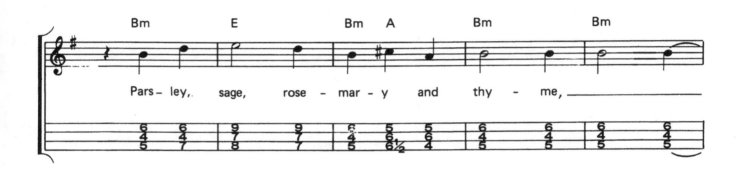

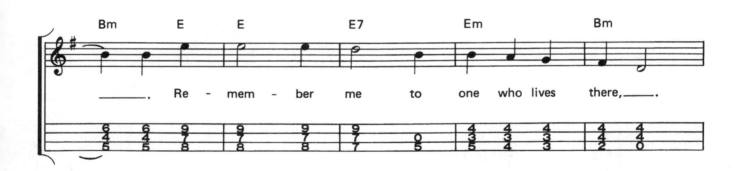

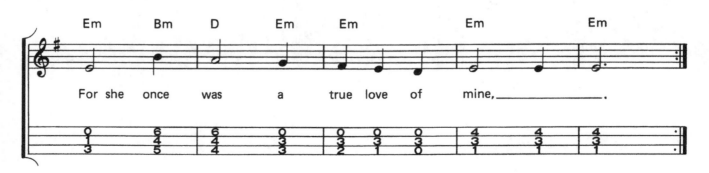

Scarborough Fair

Are you going to Scarborough Fair?
  Parsley, sage, rosemary and thyme.
Remember me to one who lives there,
For she once was a true love of mine.

Tell her to make me a good cambric shirt.
  Parsley, sage, rosemary and thyme.
Without no lace and no fancy stitching,
And then she'll be a true love of mine.

Tell her to plow me an acre of ground.
  Parsley, sage, rosemary and thyme.
Then sow it o'er with spices of all kinds,
And then she'll be a true iove of mine.

So if you're going to Scarborough Fair.
  Parsley, sage, rosemary and thyme.
Remember me to one who lives there,
For she once was a true love of mine.

Sir John "Lusty" Packington was one of Queen Elizabeth the I'st many men in waiting. It seems that he foolishly made a bet to swim the Thames River from London to Greenwich (some distance in a very polluted river) for 3,000 pounds Sterling. The Queen wisely called off the swim, but some court musician thought the theme worthy of a song. Quite a good song actually. I play it moderately fast and forcefully.

"Packington's Pound"

Aeolian Em
(D D B E)

Elizabethan Lute Tune

177

"Greensleeves"

English Lute Song
Elizabethan

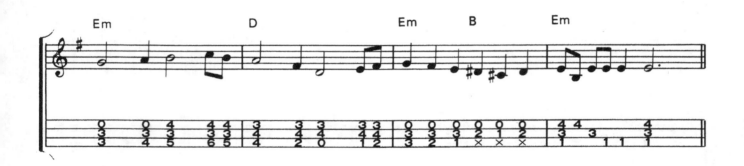

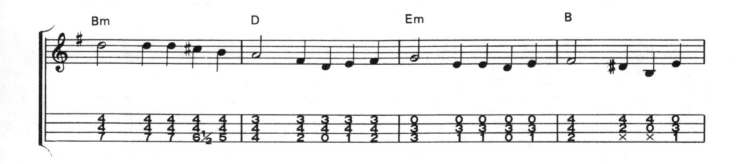

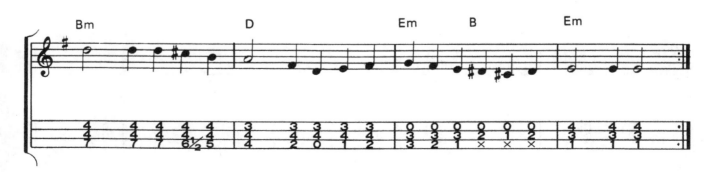

179

APPENDIX #1:
IMPORTANT TERMS AND SYMBOLS

||: :|| : means repeat exactly the passage between these bars.

X: appearing in the dulcimer tablature means that string is not to be played.

Triplet: (♩♩♩) or (♩♩♩³): a group of three notes played in the time normally given to two notes of the same time value.

Fine: the end.

Tie or slur: (⌒ or ⌣): hold the notes so connected for the total time their combined values represent—treat them as one.

Slide: (s): the sound produced when you strike a note and move to a higher or lower note without lifting your finger.

Hammer-on: (h): the sound produced when you bring your finger down forcefully on a note above the one originally struck. Your finger actually hammers out the tone without any picking occurring.

Pull-off: (p): the sound produced when you pull your finger off and back from a fretted noted, actually plucking the string with the fretting finger.

Double-mordent: a hammer-on followed by a pull-off, or vise versa, without any picking occurring in between (usually done in a series of rapid trills, a series of triplet notes being sounded).

Harmonic: clear bell like tones produced when you just barely rest your finger above one of the nodes (3rd, 4th, 7th, 11th, 14th frets) and strike the strings.

Tremelo: steady repetition or rapid strumming of a note or a chord to produce a tremulous, continuous sound. The pick rides atop the strings.

Keytone: the note which determines what key the instrument is tuned in.

APPENDIX #2:
READING MUSIC AND TIME VALUES

The dulcimer is a modal instrument, divided into a diatonic or 7 tone system. Unfortunately most music (at least modern Western music) is built around the Chromatic or 12 tone system. Therefore it is important to know a little about reading music, since eventually you'll want to play songs which aren't already scored out for you in dulcimer tablature.

Here's what one chromatic octave looks like in musical notation, with the names of the notes written below.

| C | C#
Db | D | D#
Eb | E | F | F#
Gb | G | G#
Ab | A | A#
Bb | B | C |

Music is just like any other language. You have to learn the alphabet before you can read it. Once you can recognize the notes, half the battle is over. Next you need to concentrate on learning to tell the count each note should receive; i.e. to tell whether it's a whole, or a half, or quarter note, etc. So you must also learn to recognize time signatures. So here's a bit of information on both these areas.

Note values, the time alloted to a single note, are as follows:

o = whole note; receives 4 beats.

= half note; receives 2 beats.

= quarter note; receives 1 beat

= eighth note; receives 1/2 beat, or half the time of a quarter note.

= sixteenth note; 1/2 of an eighth note ( ), or 1/4 of a quarter note.

A <u>dotted note</u> receives half again as long a count as its note value.

Rests receive the following counts:

= whole note rest;   = half note rest;   = eighth note rest   = quarter note rest;

<u>Triplets:</u> a group of three notes played in the equivalent time of two notes of the same kind.

<u>Counting the rhythm of a measure:</u> Part of the secret to playing a dulcimer, or any instrument, is to get your foot tapping out a steady rhythm in the correct time signature. Here are a few measures portrayed using a verbal count to help you join note value with the basic time.

<u>Time Signatures</u> occur directly after the treble clef (𝄞) symbol and tell you how to count the song; i.e. how many beats each measure will receive. Here are some common signatures:

C or $\frac{4}{4}$ = four beats per measure (Typical reel) Count: 1, 2, 3, 4

$\frac{3}{4}$ = three beats (Standard waltz or minuet time.) Count: 1, 2, 3/ 1, 2, 3.

$\frac{2}{4}$ = two beats (Standard polka.) Count: 1, 2/ 1, 2.

$\frac{6}{4}$ = six beats, counted: 1, 2, 3, 4, 5, 6/ 1, 2, 3, 4, 5, 6.

$\frac{6}{8}$ = six beats, (Typical jig.) usually grouped in two sets of three, counted: 1, 2, 3; 1, 2, 3/ 1, 2, 3; 1, 2, 3.

$\frac{12}{8}$ = twelve beats, usually grouped as four sets of three, counted:

1, 2, 3; 1, 2, 3; 1, 2, 3; 1, 2, 3/ 1, 2, 3; 1, 2, 3; 1, 2, 3; 1, 2, 3. (Typical slide.)

182

You may find it handy to know what notes make up which chords when you wish to figure

out fingering patterns and chords not given in the following charts.

C = C, E, G   F = F, A, C   B = B, D#, F#
C7 = C, E, G, Bb   F7 = F, A, C, D#   B7 = B, D#, F#, A
Cm = C, D#, G   Fm = F, G#, C   Bm = B, D, F#
Cm7 = C, D#, G, B   Fm7 = F, G#, C, D#   Bm7 = B, D, F#, A
Cm6 = C, D#, G, A

C# = C#, G#, G   F# = F#, A#, C#
C#7 = C#, C#, F, B   F#7 = F#, A#, C#, E
C#m = C#, G#, F, B   F#m = F#, A, C#
C#m7 = C#, G#, E, B   F#m7 = F#, A, C#, E
C#m6 = C#, G#, E, A#

D = D, F#, A   G = G, B, D
D7 = D, F#, A, C   G7 = G, B, D, F
Dm = D, F, A   Gm = G, Bb, D
Dm7 = D, F, A, C   Gm7 = G, Bb, D, F
Dm6 = D, F, A, B

E = E, G#, B   A = A, C#, E
E7 = E, G#, B, D   A7 = A, C#, E, G
Em = E, G, B   Am = A, C, E
Em7 = E, G, B, D   Am7 = A, C, E, G

Here are a couple of common chord patterns:

I	IV	V	VIm		I	VIm	IIm7	V7
C,	F,	G,	Am		C,	Am,	Dm7,	G7
G,	C,	D,	Em		G,	Em,	Am7,	D7
D,	G,	A,	Bm		D,	Bm,	Em7,	A7
A,	D,	E,	Fm		A,	F#m,	Bm7,	E7
E,	A,	B,	Cm		E,	C#m,	F#m7,	B7

183

APPENDIX #3:
MAJOR AND MINOR SCALES

A **scale** is simply a succession of seven notes arranged in a preordained series of whole and half steps. The first note of these seven toned patterns determines the name of the **key** the scale represents. The order of the whole and half steps between these seven notes determines what kind of a scale we have—major or minor. Remember that Western music is built on the 12 tones of the Chromatic Octave:

C	C#	D	D#	E	F	F#	G	G#	A	A#	B	C
STEPS: ½	½	½	½	½	½	½	½	½	½	½	½	

A scale represents 7 of these 12 possibilities arranged in a pre-established order, starting arbitrarily from any one of the twelve notes. The major scale of C starts at the C note; the minor scale of D starts with the D note. By knowing where you are starting and what scale pattern you want to follow you can always count off the proper full step and half step divisions to figure out what notes are included in the scale you are using.

A <u>major</u> scale <u>always</u> <u>follows</u> <u>the</u> <u>pattern</u>:

		full		full	1/2 step	full		full		full	1/2 step	
(C scale):	C		D		E	F	G		A		B	C
(D scale):	D		E		F♯	G	A		B		C♯	D
(7 steps):		1		2		3	4		5	6		7

<u>Note: the dulcimer fretboard automatically lays out a major scale starting with the open string and walking straight up to the 7th or octave fret, as long as you include the 6 1/2 fret.</u>

Dulcimer Fretboard:

T						(½ + ½)	
A	full	full	1/2	full	full	full	1/2
B							

(6 ½)
fret

The minor scale always flattens the third note.

				(third)					
C minor :	C	D	E♭	F	G	A	B	C	
D minor :	D	E	F	G	A	B	C♯	D	
	1	2	3♭	4	5	6	7	8	

Because the dulcimer fretboard is laid out with its series of whole and half-steps, it is often impossible to play a minor scale, and particularly the minor scale of the key you are tuned in. It is quite possible to play other minor keys out of the open tuning however. For instance in the D Mixolydian tuning we can readily play in Em and Bm because we have the proper notes.

			(flat 3rd)					
E minor :	E	F♯	G	A	B	C♯	D	E
B minor :	B	C♯	D	E	F♯	G♯	A♯	B

(Note : for the Bm scale in a D tuning we find G# at the 6 1/2 fret on the middle string, and skip the A# entirely--thereby successfully fudging the scale and playing in the key of Bm.)

Here are all the major scales with their relative minor scales beside them. Below I've written out a few of the more commonly used keys so that you can see the major-minor scales side by side. **You must remember two things about major-minor systems:**

1.) You find the relative minor scale by going to the sixth (6th) note in the major scale. This automatically tells you what key the relative minor scale will be.

KEY OF C:	C	D	E	F	G	A	B	C
	1	2	3	4	5	6	7	8

So for the key of C, A is the 6th note and Am becomes the relative minor to C-major.

2.) Once you determine what key your relatived minor scale will be, you need only call the major scale of that key (in this case A), and then flatten the third in that scale to derive the notes found in the minor scale (Am). **A major scale becomes a minor scale when you lower the third note in that scale by 1/2 step (i.e. you flatten the third).**

KEY OF A:	A	B	C#	D	E	F#	G#	A
	1	2	3	4	5	6	7	8
KEY OF Am:	A	B	C	D	E	F#	G#	A

(3rd flattened)

(Note: You can reverse the process, look at the third note in a minor scale to determine the relative major key.)

MAJOR	:	RELATIVE MINOR	MAJOR	:	RELATIVE MINOR
C	:	Am	G	:	Em
Db	:	Bbm	Ab	:	Fm
D	:	Bm	A	:	F#m
Eb	:	Cm	Bb	:	Gm
E	:	C#m	B	:	Abm
F	:	Dm			

Here are a few major-minor scales to let you see what they look like. Clearly not all the scales are playable on the dulcimer out of any single tuning. But as we've seen throughout this book, certain minor scales can be easily played out of major modal tunings and so offer many possible song variations or key transformations. The minor keys are very haunting and often more emotionally moving than their relative majors. Play around with them a little to see for yourself.

Major & Relative Minor Scales

Key C   Am

Notes: C D E F G A B C : A B C D E F# G# A
                                         (3♭)

Key D   Bm

Notes: D E F# G A B C# D : B C# D E F# G# A# B

Key G   Em

Notes: G A B C D E F# G : E F# G A B C# D# E

Key A   F#m

Notes: A B C# D E F# G# A : F# G# A B C# D# E# F#

Key E   C#m

Notes: E F# G# A B C# D# E : C# D# E F# G# A# B# C#

Key F   Dm

Notes: F G A B♭ C D E F : D E F G A B C# D

Mixolydian Mode: Chords For Key Of D*(C & E)

(Key D / Key C / Key E)
(DD A D: CC G C: EE B E)

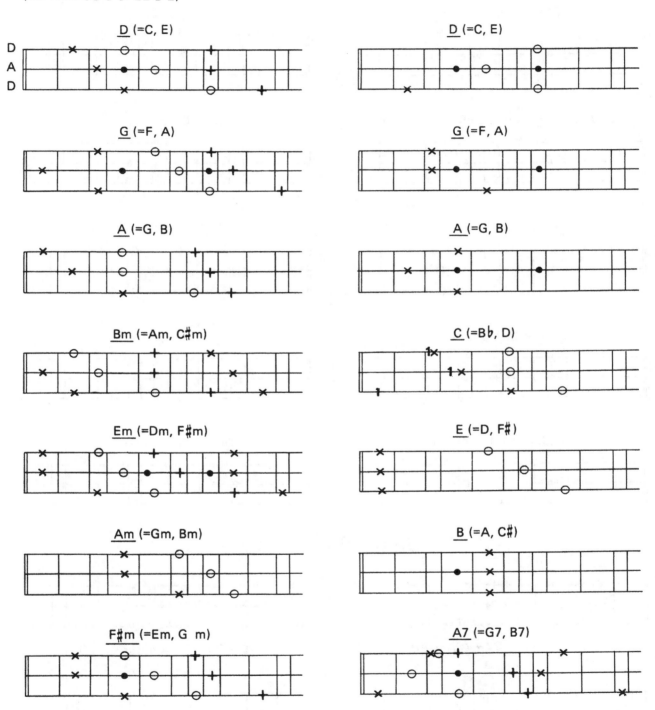

Read symbols (+, ○, ✕) as a group from right to left to make a chord. Each group makes up one possible fingering pattern equivalent to the full chord indicated. Only a few partial chords are included here.

Two important ideas must be understood here. 1.) With all chords in the Mixolydian mode the bass note and the melody note may be inverted (i.e., positions exchanged) and the chord remains the same.

Mixolydian Mode: Chords For Key Of D*(C & E)

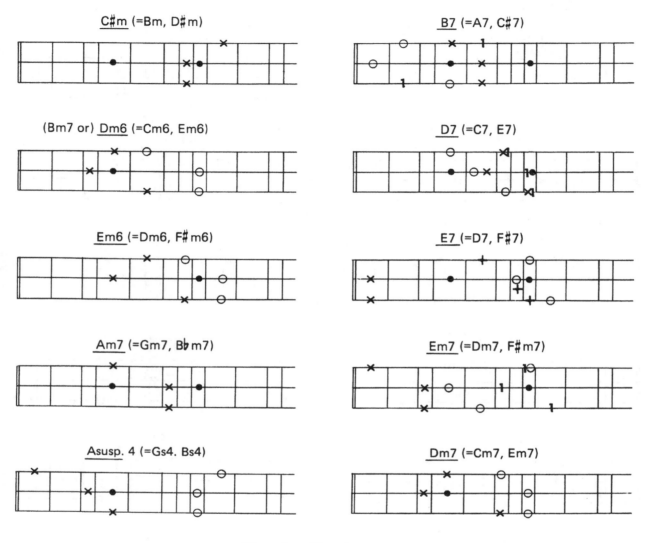

C#m (=Bm, D#m)

B7 (=A7, C#7)

(Bm7 or) Dm6 (=Cm6, Em6)

D7 (=C7, E7)

Em6 (=Dm6, F#m6)

E7 (=D7, F#7)

Am7 (=Gm7, B♭m7)

Em7 (=Dm7, F#m7)

Asusp. 4 (=Gs4. Bs4)

Dm7 (=Cm7, Em7)

Basic Patterns:

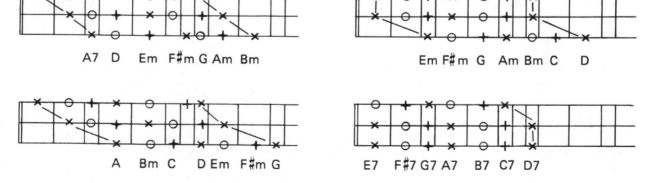

A7 D   Em F#m G Am Bm

Em F#m G   Am Bm C   D

A   Bm C   D Em F#m G

E7   F#7 G7 A7   B7 C7 D7

2.) Fingerings remain the same when you are tuned in different keys; only the name of the chord changes relative to the key you're in. I have indicated in parenthesis the new chord names for the same fingerings when you change from the key of D to the keys of C and E.

188

New Ionian Mode: Chords For Key G (F, A)

DD G D: (C C F C): (E E A E)

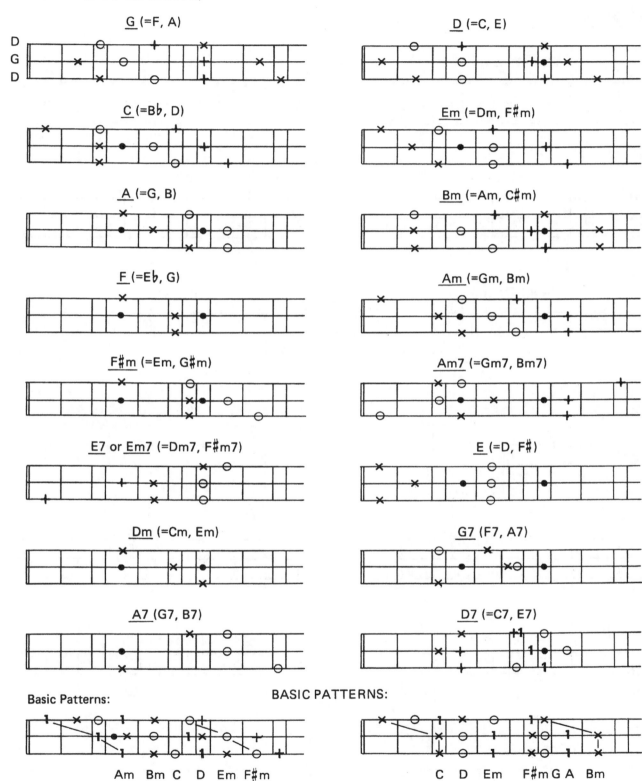

189

Aeolian Mode: Chords For Key Of Em (Dm, Cm)

(Key Em/Dm/Cm)
(D D B E / C C A D / B♭B♭G C)

Em(Dm,Cm)

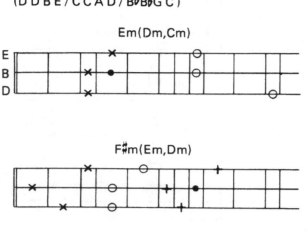

E(D,C)

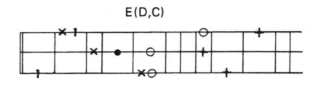

F#m(Em,Dm)

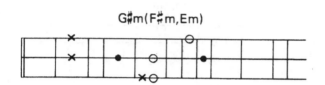

F#(E,D)

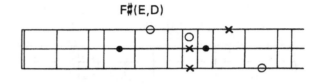

G#m(F#m,Em)

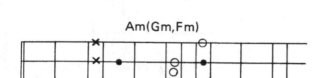

G(F,E♭)

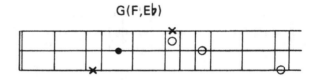

Am(Gm,Fm)

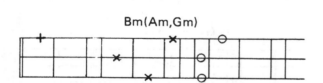

A(G,F)

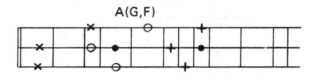

Bm(Am,Gm)

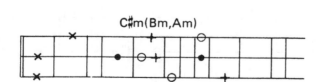

B(A,G)

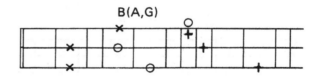

C#m(Bm,Am)

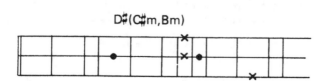

C#(B,A) (partial)

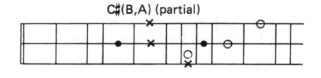

D#(C#m,Bm)

D(C,B♭)

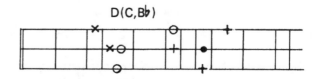

Aeolian Mode: Chords For Key Of Em (Dm, Cm)

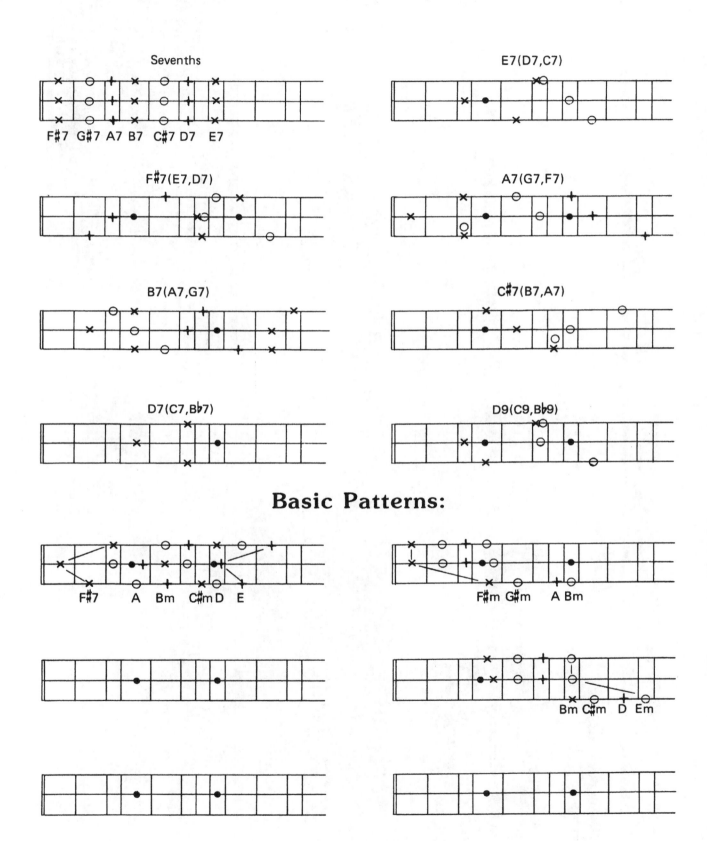

Basic Patterns:

Photo by Mark Biggs

THE OTHER MODES: New Dorian & Lydian

There are four other modes besides the three we have looked at so far: the Dorian, Lydian, Locrian and Phrygian Modes. In reality however, only the Dorian and the Lydian Modes are ever used. I occasionally play in the New Dorian since it offers a minor sound quite different from the Aeolian and equally pleasing to my ears. However, I suggest you experiment with these other Modes only after you feel comfortable with the Mixolydian, Ionian and Aeolian Modes. Here's how to tune into two of them.

Called the "mountain minor", the **Dorian Mode** possesses an irregular minor scale with a flattened sixth as well as a flatted third like the normal minor scale. Once considered the "bestower of wisdom and clarity" it is sometimes used in traditional British and American folk music (particularly in the 17th Century).

Tuning:

To get into the **Dorian Mode**, tune your bass string to the chosen keytone. Next fret it at the fourth and tune the middle string one octave above this tone. Finally fret the bass at the third and tune the melody string to this tone, one octave higher.

To tune into the **New Dorian from the Mixolydian**, fret the melody string at the first fret and tune the bass string to this tone one octave lower. The middle string remains unchanged. From the Aeolian Mode, simple fret the middle string at the third fret and tune it to the exact same tone as the melody string played open.

DORIAN MODE:	Melody	Middle	Bass	Key
	DD	E	A	(Am)
	CC	D	G	(Gm)
	GG	A	D	(DM)
	(1)	(9)	(5)	

NEW DORIAN:				
	DD	A	E	(Am)
	CC	G	D	(Gm)
	EE	B	F#	(Bm)
	(1)	(5)	(9)	

To get into the **Lydian Mode** tune the bass string to the desired keytone. Fret the bass at the first and tune the melody string one octave above this tone. Fret the bass at the fourth and tune the middle to this tone one octave higher.

To tune into the **Lydian Mode from the New Ionian**, simply fret the middle string at the third and lower the bass string one full step to this same tone; check the bass against the melody string fretted at the sixth.

LYDIAN MODE:	Melody	Middle	Bass	Key
	DD	G	C	(C)
	CC	F	Bb	(Bb)
	EE	A	D	(D)
	(1)	(4)	(6)	

ARRANGING YOUR SONGS BY MODES:
How To Fall Through the Modes With Ease

Once you have begun to build a repertoire of songs in several different modes you may find it a nuisance to be constantly retuning from one mode to another. Likewise when you play with friends or perform in public it is important not to waste time or to exhaust the audience's patience by constantly switching from one mode or key to another. Therefore a little planning is in order. If you will arrange your songs by keys and modes, you can plan to start at the highest key and modal tuning and fall down through your songlist without ever having to retune more than one string. I usually begin in the Aeolian Mode, fall through the New Dorian into the Mixolydian and end with the New Ionian Mode. Such a maneuver looks like this:

AEOLIAN:	DD	B	E	(Em)	or	CC	A	D	(Dm)
NEW DORIAN:	DD	A	E	(Am)	or	CC	G	D	(Gm)
MIXOLYDIAN:	DD	A	D	(D)	or	CC	G	C	(C)
NEW IONIAN:	DD	G	D	(G)	or	CC	F	C	(F)

A little forethought can save a lot of time and energy and even a few broken strings, as well as make playing songs in different modes much easier and more fun.

FAREWELL AND ADIEU

Music is as much the fine art of listening as it is of playing; it is as much the space between the notes as it is the sound of the notes themselves. Always listen to yourself when you play just as you would listen to someone whose playing you respect or as you would listen to a favorite record: with careful attention and personal involvement. When you make music with friends, which you should do as often as possible, listen to the total sound as well as to your contribution. The more you hear the more in tune with everyone you'll become and the better the music will sound. Try not to get too wrapped up in the physical act of playing. For the longest time I was consumed with the "act" of playing; swept away by the desire to perfect my "technique". I see this happening with so many dulcimer players. Their main concern isn't with the music, but with learning some new lick or perfecting some particular song instead of trying to feel what they are playing; instead of trying to express what they are feeling through their music. Music is nothing but a mathematical exercise or an armchair athletic event if the emotion is absent. If you aren't ultimately playing to express your feelings then you might as well slip on a tape and go for a jog around the block. Music is a miraculous encapsulation of emotion; an encapsulation which must be released anew each time by you, the musician, the sound-magician. It's the emotion which keeps music fresh and intangibly ever-present; it's the emotion contained within a song that keeps it meaningful and worth preserving. A good song is a fine friend, and you'd never treat a good friend indifferently. Feeling and texture, the means by which you express your emotions in the arrangement of a song, these are everything in music.

Perseverance is one of the keys to becoming a good musician capable of expressing your feelings. Try to practice at least fifteen or twenty minutes in a row per day; there's nothing so frustrating and ultimately discouraging as having to relearn the same old lessons over and over. You have to play until you "know" your music well enough to forget it and to begin to allow your hands and heart to work their magic. Persevere, don't get frustrated, keep the dulcimer something enjoyable, and practically everything you'll want to do musically will become possible in time. Always share your knowledge and ideas with your friends and acquaintances— you can only gain by doing so.

By all means feel free to write me c/o: R.R. #3 Box 367B/Galena, Mo. 65656 (be sure to enclose a stamped self-addressed envelope.) I'll be happy to answer any questions to the best of my ability. And thanks for reading this far...I sincerely hope this book has been of some small help.

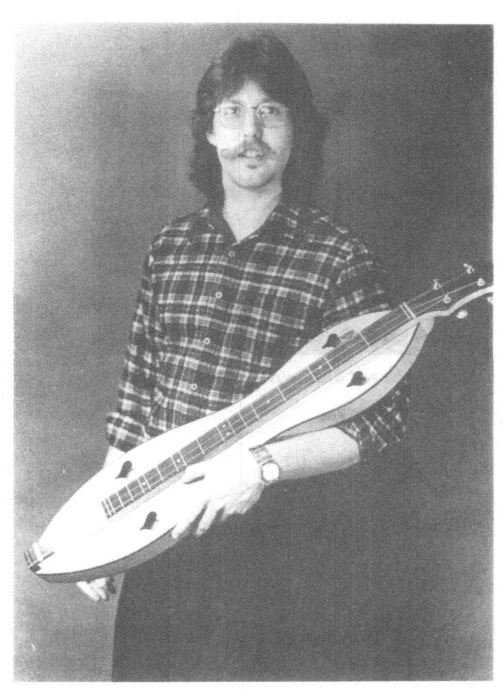